Acclaim for *Prodigal*

"What a story—a real page-turner! In it, Wynn Thompson reveals a most amazing journey from childhood sexual abuse to drug addiction, jail, a brush with fame as a singer, and his inevitable plunge into intractable sexual addiction and homosexual behavior. The bonus—an appendix on the causes and path to freedom from homosexual confusion—is icing on the cake. I highly recommend this moving journal of a broken and then redeemed life."

—**Dr. David Kyle Foster**, MDiv, DMin; author; executive director of Mastering Life Ministries; producer and director of award-winning *Pure Passion* TV program

"If you only read one book about how same-sex attraction develops in the life of a child and how God can transform the broken, this is your book!"

—**Carol L. Wagstaff Groen**, MA; executive director Living Stones Ministries; author of *Reclaim, Restore, and Rebuild: Hope for Families Impacted by Sexual Brokenness*

"As I was reading my way through Wynn's story, I was struck by the honesty and the candid insights he shares along the way. It is powerful when you look back and can see what you missed on the journey but also how God was working. Wynn's is a story of redemption that has you asking how you come back from that level of brokenness. As you read layer by layer, you see how God restores a life. Wynn's story is a reminder of how we are deceived by our circumstances, and yet God can shine a light in the darkest of places. This story is one I would highly recommend for all to embrace and learn from. Wynn has woven in the wisdom that comes from a journey with God, and I

believe churches everywhere can benefit from this kind of resource. I also believe this story of hope and insight will help those who are facing and have faced similar heartache. My friendship with Wynn and our partnership with his ministry has allowed me to see his integrity, vulnerability, and wisdom firsthand. As he takes you through his journey, you get to experience the highs and lows that he has experienced. This book is a must-read as I know it is going to help those who read it. Thank you, Jesus, for working so powerfully in Wynn's life."

—**Rev. Chris Swart**, senior pastor of Life Church
Somerset West, Western Cape, South Africa

"Some special people possess the courage to change their lifestyles and become a blessing to many. Wynn is one of these giants. He was always straightforward and sincere but never pushy about sharing his story. Gradually, it came to light. It was as a video producer that Wynn showed me his talent and creative flair. Behind this was a man who had journeyed through suffering, doubts, and rejection. Faith in Christ had restored the unmendable. He has always been a person of warmth and generosity. This willingness to help others who had been in similar situations to his own has grown into a significant and powerful work. Wynn has courageously taken his convictions forward and made full use of his hard-learned wisdom. He takes risks, tries new ideas, and keeps being creative. All of this is backed up with a strong faith that allows him to be close to where people are, walking with them on their sinuous paths. Whether our background is similar to his or not, we all have something to learn from him."

—**Paul Marsh**, president of Jeunesse en Mission Suisse
Romande; international executive vice president of
Marriage Week International; chair of the Family Couple and
Singles network, European Evangelical Alliance

"From the minute I started reading Wynn Cameron Thompson's memoir of his journey to freedom, I was captivated and many times moved to tears. Never before has the very fabric of our society been under such attack and at such risk. With teenage suicides and anxiety levels soaring, his story and testimony is such an important beacon of hope and restoration in a landscape of growing abuse, brokenness, and identity confusion. The transformative power of his redemptive narrative unfolds, and he shares with such honesty, vulnerability, and courage. So many liberating truths have been captured in this story. His testimony will bring many onto their own journey to finding freedom and having their wholeness restored."

—**Gavin Wiseman**, development manager, South Africa

"Prodigal is a book of hope! As the reader engages, it quickly opens the heart to deeper understanding, compassion, and empathy for others. Not only is this book for those who have experienced shame coming from deep wounds and brokenness caused by abuse from trusted others, or for those who have made wrong choices and decisions from youthful lusts and ignorance, but it is also for the deeply religious pharisee in all of us. Wynn's honesty, transparency, and vulnerability exposes the reader's pride and barriers that prevent a follower of Christ from loving others as Jesus commands His followers to do. I have been privileged to know and work alongside Wynn for the past fourteen years and can truly say Wynn loves others with the love of Christ that he has been shown. His example has transformed my life and given me a greater revelation of the Father's love for me."

—**Brett Martin**, Campus Missionary, Chi Alpha affiliate, Restoring Wholeness staff and board member

"In his book, *Prodigal: A Journey to Freedom from Abuse and Addiction,* Wynn Thompson presents us with a raw, tough to chew at times, story that doesn't always go down easy. You may be left to digest and process it for a while, but the spiritual value of Wynn's story makes reading it 100 percent worthwhile. Jesus and the healing and restoration He offers to all is evident throughout *Prodigal*. And if ingesting such a raw story brings greater value than a boiled-down and doctored-up story, then sign me up. The spiritual value gained from reading this book will leave you with no regrets."

—**Kai Eilert,** Lead Pastor of Central City Assembly, Tucson, Arizona

Prodigal

A Journey to Freedom from
Abuse and Addiction

Wynn Cameron Thompson

with Lori Conser

Prodigal: A Journey to Freedom from Abuse and Addiction

Published by Wheatmark®
2030 East Speedway Boulevard, Suite 106
Tucson, Arizona 85719 USA
www.wheatmark.com

ISBN: 978-1-62787-914-9 (paperback)
ISBN: 978-1-62787-915-6 (ebook)
LCCN: 2021917949

Front cover photo by Brett Martin
Cover and book design by Lori Conser

Bulk-ordering discounts are available through Wheatmark, Inc.
For more information, email orders@wheatmark.com
or call 1-888-934-0888.

To Shae — God bless you!

To my wife, Judi,
the love of my life and my dearest friend,
the one who has stood by me all these years.

To my family and those who have
become my family:
you have supported me through the good times
and the bad.

For those seeking hope and freedom from
shame, wounding, and brokenness:
this book is for you.

I hope you'll be able to be blessed reading my book. May God always supply all your needs — Body, Soul & Spirit,

Wynn

ACKNOWLEDGMENTS

I am overwhelmed by the outpouring of help to get this manuscript published. There are so many who donated to my GoFundMe campaign. Your generosity made this all possible.

Thank you Lori Conser for your help, patience, and tenacity in working with me over the last three years. Your God-given talent is amazing. I praise God for you every day!

For everyone who contributed their time and wisdom in helping *Prodigal* become a better book, especially Jeannette Howard, Dr. David Kyle Foster, Carol Wagstaff Groen, Paul Marsh, Pastor Chris Swart, Gavin Wiseman, Pastor Kai Eilert, Katherine Salas, Mark Dupaul, Rachel Pye, and Daniel Sellstrom, your help, reviews, and critiques were magnanimous.

God bless you all!

CONTENTS

FOREWORD

Wynn loomed over the desk where I sat. It was 2013, and we were in Irvine, California, where I had been speaking, as it transpired, at the final Exodus International Conference. He flashed an engaging smile as he thrust a copy of my latest book toward me and waited for my rather illegible signature. As we chatted, it became clear that enthusiasm for life and love for Jesus oozed out of every pore of the man's being and I quickly warmed to him. I have followed Wynn's ministry and personal life with interest since that time, and I am honored that he has asked me to write the foreword for his book, *Prodigal: A Journey to Freedom from Abuse and Addiction.*

I enjoy listening to audiobooks while doing something practical like gardening or working on my van conversion. My preferred genre is the political thriller or detective story, something to occupy my brain while my body engages in the functional. I wouldn't, however, listen to a James Bond novel, preferring to watch that action-packed story on the big screen. Wynn's book could be a screen-play for such a film!

Prodigal reads more like a regular novel than the typical format favored by most Christian testimonials. He does not follow the well-established method of describing one's pre-Christian life in a sketchy, ill-focused style before dedicating most of the book to the impact a conversion to Jesus has had on the individual. Wynn doesn't deal in fuzzy outlines but declares his story in bold sweeping strokes for all to see. His storytelling is realistically vivid, refusing to offer vague descriptions of abuse and its emotional and physical impact on this young boy raised in a Christian family. As the victim turned hunter, we read of Wynn's life as a narcissistic sexual predator hoping that drugs and alcohol and a life in Hollywood will protect him from the vast gamut of emotions trying to find a voice. It is a life of hedonistic self-destruction and yet, through it all, runs the thin thread of a Father's love calling him home. After a doctor's dire warning, the thirty-two-year-old Wynn eventually moves out of the city.

> Leaving LA, the drug culture, and the rat race helped, but it wasn't enough. I wanted out of the gay lifestyle and everything it stood for. It was that simple. I had finally come to the point where I really was sick and tired of being sick and tired. I was at a breaking point, and something had to change.
>
> There was only one answer, and I knew it was Jesus. Had He really waited for me all these years to come to Him?

The second half of the book recounts how the Lord graciously dealt with the foundational hurt experienced by the young Wynn, and his developing attitudes, false beliefs, and subsequent behavior that evolved from such pain. Although many of Wynn's experiences are, thankfully, unknown to me, I could certainly identify with his need to recognize these erroneous drivers that fueled his life and expose them in the presence of our dear Lord. It is only in allowing God's truth in those inner places that any of us can hope to walk upright in the truth of who we truly are. Wynn skillfully uses a few events over several years to highlight how ingrained some of our broken responses are and how they, if not addressed, can hinder our maturation both personally and ministerially.

This is, without doubt, the story of the prodigal who not only finds his way home but learns how to live and flourish with his Father in the "big house." Allowing the Father to wash, clothe, and direct him, Wynn has used his past for Kingdom purposes, enabling many other prodigals to come home.

A word of caution. The novel-like technique will, no doubt, inspire the hope of healing to many readers who have experienced abuse of various kinds and have made poor life choices. However, the style may also prove too much for some. Read it for yourself before you consider giving it to others. Experientially, you may have little mutuality with Wynn, but I can guarantee you will find great commonality when it comes to the shared issues of surrender, humility, and obedience.

For some forty-plus years, Wynn has trusted his Father to change him from the inside out. We are the beneficiaries of this often deeply painful journey, and for that I am grateful. Wynn Cameron Thompson's testimony is proof that the Lord does confer *a crown of beauty instead of ashes, the oil of joy instead of mourning, and a garment of praise instead of a spirit of despair* (Isaiah 61:3), and that Wynn is most certainly an *oak of righteousness, a planting of the LORD for the display of his splendor.*

—Jeanette Howard, speaker and author of *Out of Egypt, Into the Promised Land,* and *Dwelling in the Land*

AUTHOR'S NOTE

Over the past twenty years, people have asked me, "Have you ever written a book about your life and adventures?"

They are curious about how a man who lived most of his life addicted to homosexuality, pornography, drugs, and alcohol can change. My Christian brothers and sisters understand the transformation in my life is a work of Christ's redemption, but they are still curious about how it all happened. In other words, they want to hear my stories.

To be honest, I've never really thought about writing a book because so many books have already been published on topics like dysfunctional families, sexual abuse, fragmented and confused identities, and same-sex attraction. But the question kept coming up, so I started praying, "Lord, if you want me to write a book, please show me by sending someone to help me."

Later, my friend Michael Padrick coached me in writing out two chapters, which I shared with Lori Conser, a woman who attends my church and works in publishing.

"Have you made any more progress on your book?" she asked one day after church.

"No, not a bit," I said.

Lori told me she had been praying and sensed God was leading her to help. I was overwhelmed.

And so the process of recording my memoirs began. After working on this for three years, I have come to realize how cathartic this exercise has been. I am so thankful Lori listened to our Father and followed through.

I want to make something clear from the beginning. I have not written this book to make a political statement on homosexuality. However, you do need to know where I stand on this issue. I believe God has designed humankind for intimate companionship with Him forever. He made us—male and female—in His image so that we can reflect His glory. Men and women are different but complementary beings. We are not only made from one flesh (the woman from the man in creation), but we come from a one-flesh union (the man from the woman in birth). When we fit together as part of the sexual union in marriage, we become one flesh again, allowing for fruitfulness. This fruitfulness is shown on the physical level by having children, but it is also spiritual by showing God's intended design to be fruitful in everything we do (see Matthew 19:4–6, Ephesians 5:31–33).

Homosexual relationships do not fall into this intended design. Neither does any other kind of sexual brokenness, including sexual abuse and molestation, family dysfunction, adultery, incest, addiction to pornography, and heterosexual sex outside of marriage.

In the end, our view on this issue hinges on how we

answer the following question: should God change for humanity, or should humanity change for God?

Humanity is finite; God is infinite. I believe we should change for God, not the other way around.

Of course, this question only makes sense if we believe in God and His absolute truth. If you don't believe in absolute truth, then anything goes. This relative philosophy is playing out in our world, and it almost took me down. What I found was that while doing whatever pleased me satisfied my immediate cravings, it eventually led to confusion, brokenness, and destruction. It was only by choosing to conform myself to God's design that I was able to become whole through the process and help of the Lord.

This is my story about my journey to wholeness. Except for some condensing and combining for brevity sake and a few name changes to protect the privacy of individuals, it is how I remember it. I can honestly say that once I was blind, but now I see. The moments described in the following pages helped to define and then change the trajectory of my life. I hope that by reading about them, you will turn to Jesus for your answer in whatever struggles you may have. May you be inspired and encouraged to push forward and not give up until you experience the true deliverance you are seeking.

I love what Mark Batterson wrote in his book *Soul Print*: "Without the ability to remember yesterday, the ability to imagine tomorrow would become meaningless . . . Our memories can either empower us to live by faith or imprison us to live by fear." The moments reflected in this book are from my yesterdays, and God has used them to make my life meaningful.

When we get sick and tired of being sick and tired, when we are willing to do anything for our healing, something wonderful happens. We give up control, throw in the towel, and humble ourselves before God. He has been waiting for us all along, ready to do what no man can do: help us experience His original intent for our lives. Such revelation is a life-defining moment. We begin to walk away from our false selves and discover our true selves. Are you ready?

Lori Conser and Wynn, 2018.

Michael Padrick and Wynn.

"We'll need your car keys, wallet, jewelry—any personal items," the guard said.

I knew the drill all too well and had purposefully left everything at home—even my car keys. My brother, Brian, had driven me to the county jail, where I was sentenced to spend the next three months.

"We're praying for you," Brian had reassured me as we stood outside the gray stone building. Then he gave me a brisk hug before saying goodbye. "God hasn't abandoned you," he said. "You'll get through this."

I knew he was right—at least I thought I did. But it felt as though my old life—my old self—was reaching up from the chasm where I had left it seven years before, trying desperately to grab me and pull me under.

You'll never be any good. God doesn't want your kind in His kingdom, a familiar voice taunted me. *He's abandoned you just like you've abandoned Him so many times. Why don't you quit this charade?*

PART ONE

Lost Innocence

1

STOLEN

"You can't ride it," Marlane said. "You're too small."

Marlane was a bossy ten-year-old who lived two doors down from me. She had just received a purple bicycle with long handlebars for her birthday and had been riding it up and down the street several times before stopping to give me a closeup view.

"I can so ride it," I said, looking with wonder at the large purple machine. I was only six and had never ridden a bike before. But I was confident I could manage it better than Marlane.

Popping her Bazooka bubble gum, Marlane shrugged and then began pushing her bike up the steep hill at the end of our street. I raced along beside her, wondering what she was up to. Once reaching the top, she pointed down the hill. "Okay, you can go down this hill so you won't have to pedal," she explained, breathless. "But I'm coming with you."

"I can ride it by myself," I said.

She shook her head. "No way. It's my bike. I'm either coming with you, or you can forget it."

I nodded. It *was* her bike. With my feet planted firmly on each side, I straddled the bike while Marlane climbed onto the handlebars. Then I pushed off, struggling to keep the heavy load on the handlebars steady. The bike picked up speed, and Marlane's long, stringy hair blew in my face. What fun!

But then everything went askew. The bike picked up too much speed; the front wheel wobbled and then turned sharply sideways, throwing me and Marlane into the air.

There were no serious injuries from this mishap, only some scrapes and bruises, but I would not always be so fortunate. Eager to embrace every adventure that came my way, I never suspected any danger in the quiet neighborhood where I grew up. My only brother, Brian, was eight years older and could easily take care of a neighborhood bully should one ever come along. And my parents were loving and devoted to God. Every night as I lay in my bed, I would gaze at the living room light penetrating my partially opened doorway, comforted by the sound of their prayers.

In 1952, Los Angeles was very different from today— at least it seemed that way. This was before the mass exodus to the suburbs, when most middle-class families still lived and worked in the city. Neighborhoods felt safe, and parents thought nothing about letting their children play outside unsupervised.

I was a confident child who could entertain myself when there were no playmates around, and I often pretended to be a policeman or a fireman. But playing doctor was my favorite make-believe role. This was the game I was playing on the day in 1952 when everything turned upside down.

I was six years old on the warm summer day when I put a small plastic stethoscope around my neck, grabbed my toy doctor case, and headed out the door. Our neighborhood was an older one with small homes built in the 1920s and '30s. The houses on our side of the street were situated along the side of a hill—mostly hidden from a small child's view by tall stone support walls. On the other side of the road, the houses were at street level—visible behind small fenced-in yards.

I crossed the street and began walking along the sidewalk, looking for patients to help. Nobody was around until I came to the fourth house. Four teenage boys were standing in a huddle, passing a cigarette among themselves. They were peering at a magazine and speaking Spanish, a language I couldn't understand. Each boy was wearing jeans and T-shirts, but it was their dog that really caught my attention. It was standing at the feet of one of the boys—a muscular, rust-colored beast. I was fascinated by its powerful, protruding chest, large head, and yellow eyes. The dog was leashed by a thin rope tied around its neck, and a lanky boy was holding the other end. It was staring straight at me, its ears perked and its haunches quivering. Then it licked its chops and growled soft and low.

The boy holding the leash looked down and spoke

firmly to the dog in Spanish. Then he looked at me while taking a long drag from his cigarette.

"Hey, *chico blanco*, what're you lookin' at, eh? You like my *perro*? I don't think he likes you." He laughed.

He said something to his friends, and they laughed and yelled things at me in Spanish. Then the boy with the dog casually sauntered over with a menacing grin on his face. His dog pulled eagerly at the rope, and the boy yanked him back.

"*Sentar!*" he shouted at the dog, who obediently sat down and gazed up at the boy, panting.

The boy dropped the rope to the ground and walked toward me, while the dog remained sitting several feet back. The boy's shadow covered me as I squinted up at him. Then he reached for the small stethoscope around my neck and held it between his fingers.

"What're you doing, chico? Playing doctor?" His voice was soft and gentle.

I nodded.

He was still fondling the stethoscope around my neck when he said, "You should come with us, and we'll all play together." Then he pointed toward a cellar door on the side of his house. "We have a secret place under there. C'mon. It'll be fun."

I'm not sure if it was because playmates were hard to come by in my neighborhood or because I was impressed that older boys wanted to play with me, but for some reason, I followed him. His friends walked behind me, and the dog followed his master, the rope trailing behind him.

I stopped at the open door. The room smelled of

mildew and earth. Cobwebs fell from the low ceiling, and the filtered daylight through the open door revealed a dirt floor and several stacks of boxes and old household items piled in one of the corners. I hesitated and was pushed roughly through the doorway by a boy behind me. Once everyone was inside, the leader spoke to his friends in Spanish and started unbuckling his belt.

I froze. What was he going to do? Was he going to spank me? I was pretty sure I had done nothing to deserve a spanking, and I thought about running away, but the dog was sitting by the door, and the three other boys were blocking my way.

The leader must have noticed my fear. His unbuckled belt now hung loose in his belt loops. "You think I'm going to hit you with this? Is that what you think?" He laughed while toying playfully with the buckle. He shook his head. "A spanking is too good for a boy like you," he said, clucking his tongue and shaking his head. "Only dirty little boys like to play doctor." Then he leaned over and spoke softly. "You see how my perro obeys me? All I have to do is say one word, and he will attack. That's right. He knows he must obey me or else. My perro will kill you if I ask him to. He will do what I say. So now you must do what I say. *Comprendes*?"

I wish I could erase from my memory what happened next, and I wish I could spare you from reading about it. But this is where the root of shame began in my life, and you must know what happened to me here so that you can understand the rest of my story.

Dirty hands covered my mouth, stifling my screams,

as each boy took his turn violating me while the others pinned me down. The horror was beyond anything my young brain could comprehend, not so much because of physical pain but because of the feeling of utter helplessness. I scrambled to escape but only succeeded in grinding myself farther into the dirt as it went on and on. When they were finally finished, the leader jerked my underwear and pants up and ordered me to stand in front of him. My legs felt like they were going to collapse as he gripped my terrified face in his hands and looked down at me. Confused, bewildered, shaking, and sobbing uncontrollably, I tried not to look back. I tried hard not to think of the dirty, ugly evil that had just invaded me.

"You see, chico?" the leader said, a malicious grin playing on his young face. "We weren't going to spank you. We were just playing doctor." The other boys laughed.

Then he grabbed a fist full of my hair, forcing my gaze up. "It is good that you are afraid," he said. "Because if you ever tell anyone what just happened, me and my perro, we will find you, and we will kill you. Comprendes?"

I looked down at my feet, tears blurring my vision. He shook me violently. "Understand?"

I nodded. Then he pulled his T-shirt over his head, exposing his dark torso, and used the shirt to wipe the dirt from my face and hair. "There now, you see?" he said, showing me the dirt marks on his shirt. "You are just as good as new. Don't forget what I said. We will not forget."

~

I don't remember how I got home, but my mother must have heard me crying through the front screen door because she came rushing out and knelt as I ran into her arms. Trembling took over my body in unceasing hiccups while she tried to console me.

"Shhhh . . . shhhh," she whispered. "You're okay. I'm here. What happened? Did you hurt yourself?"

How could I tell her? What could I say? Finally, breathless and exhausted, I said, "Some big boys . . ."

She pulled me back and examined me at arm's length, her face creased with concern. "What is it, Wynn?"

"Some big boys . . ." I sobbed. "They . . ."

But I couldn't say it. I didn't even know how to say it.

"It's OK. You can tell me."

I knew I had to tell her something, so I finally said in a small voice, "Some big boys . . . they stole my toys."

Those words still ring in my head today.

They stole my toys.

They stole a lot more than that.

Dad holding me as a baby.

With Mom at Glacier Point—
Half Dome is in the background.

Mom, Brian, and me (at six) in front of our home
on Prince Street in Lincoln Heights.
My dad was taking the picture.

Me at age seven, on top of our garage on
Prince Street in Lincoln Heights, Los Angeles.

2

AFTERMATH

It's hard to know for certain all the effects the rape had on my life. Although I never told a soul about it until much later, I think my family knew something had changed; they just didn't understand the severity of it. I'm sure I must have had some bruises and soreness, but there was no bleeding, no noticeable physical damage. The injuries were more insidious, affecting the deep recesses of my thoughts, emotions, and unconscious mind.

My brother, Brian, was fourteen at the time. He was there when I ran home and cried about the boys who had stolen my toys. He saw my tear-stained face and noticed how I was too scared to come out of my room. He thought I had been bullied by older boys, and he was ready to do something about it.

"I'm gonna get your toys back," he announced, pulling me up from my bed where I had been crying. "You need to come with me."

That was the last thing I wanted to do—my lost doctor kit was long forgotten. I backed away, shaking my head violently. But Brian had a strong dose of righteous anger running through him, and he was not taking no for an answer. "You have to come," he said. "You need to show me who did it."

He was relentless, trying to convince me that he would keep me safe. He wouldn't allow them to bully me again, he said. In his anger, he was longing to do something to make it right, and I was grateful. Since my father was at work, Brian must have felt it was his role to step in and be my protector. I finally agreed to go, but he still had to encourage me along the way.

"Come on, Wynn," he said, motioning with his arm as I lingered in the walled stairwell that led up to our next-door neighbor's house. He waited for me to catch up; then he took my hand in his so that I would walk faster.

"Which house is it?" he asked.

I hesitated, then pointed out the small gray home on the other side of the street.

Brian started to cross, but I pulled back, yanking his hand and trying to resist.

He stopped and looked down at me. "We're going to do this," he said firmly.

I gave in and started walking.

When we arrived, the four boys were sitting on a small porch at the side of their house, playing some kind of game. Their dog was lying beside a middle-aged woman who was sitting in a rocking chair next to them. Three of the boys stared at us as we approached, but the one who had instigated the rape only gave us a passing glance.

Brian did all the talking. "Where's my brother's doctor

kit?" he demanded, his voice sounding unsteady and higher than normal. "We want it back!"

The woman on the porch stopped rocking and leaned forward. She spoke something in Spanish to the boys, and the leader said something back to her. Then he turned and stared at us. "We didn't steal anything," he said, glaring at me before continuing his game. The other boys started playing again too. Frustrated, my brother looked at the woman. My little plastic stethoscope was lying under her rocker. He hesitated. He was outnumbered, and the woman seemed unable—or unwilling—to get involved. So Brian took my hand, and we walked home.

~

I never saw those boys again, and the family moved away a few years later. But my fears lasted long after they were gone. From then on, I always stayed close to home and never ventured on my own down the street.

My family had a small black-and-white television set, and I spent hours watching TV shows, losing myself in the world of entertainment. My favorite show was *Superman*, which came on once a week. Superman was my hero. I would think about him every night, hoping I would become Superman in my dreams—invincible and fighting the demons that haunted me. But once sleep took over, the monsters would chase me down. I'd try to fly away like Superman, but I'd fall instead, spiraling out of control into an abyss of darkness where hideous monsters would hold me down, breathing fire into my face, clawing at me with dirty hands clamped over my mouth. Not a week went by when I could escape those nightmares.

I was no longer comforted when hearing my parents pray for me at night; my young mind was confused. *Why hadn't God protected me? Why was God mad at me?* The rape also affected me in other ways. I became interested in sexual play and would instigate simple sex games like "doctor" and "I'll show you mine if you show me yours" with other children who came to play at my house. Although some of this was normal curiosity, I became preoccupied with it to the point of near obsession.

My parents were unaware that any of this was going on. Had they known, they would have been horrified—at least that's what I thought. So I kept it hidden. Little did I know I was setting down a pattern of secrecy in my life—a pattern that would carry through to adulthood. Even at the tender age of six, two different people were beginning to emerge inside of me: the happy, outgoing child who loved to sing hymns in church and the secretive boy who was consumed with shame and guilt. To feel better, I would constantly set my mind on sexual things, unaware that this only heightened my feelings of shame and guilt. I had lost my innocence and had no idea how to get it back.[1]

On the surface, life seemed normal. But my wounds ran deep. I became an expert at hiding them, largely due to my extroverted personality. It was easy for me to perform

---

1 See Appendix: The Crisis of Sexual Identity, for information on how children form unhealthy identities and what parents can do to protect them.

and pretend to be fine most of the time, but I did act out on occasion—signs overlooked by the adults in my life. My parents were concerned that I struggled in school; reading was especially difficult for me because I was dyslexic. But this was an unknown condition in the 1950s, and I wasn't diagnosed until I was an adult. When I was a child, my teachers said I was a slow learner. My mom and dad spent extra time reading with me and trying to help, but nothing worked. I just couldn't see the letters the way they did.

When I was in the fourth grade, I was an outgoing child with lots of friends. My classroom had about twenty-five students, and we sat in vertical rows of individual desks. A smaller boy named Donny was part of the group of friends I hung out with. He was a smart kid who always seemed to win a ribbon at the science fair each year, but he was no jewel to look at. A skinny kid, Donny sat behind me and had greasy ash-blond hair that stood up at the crown of his head. He wore thick metal glasses that dropped to the end of his nose and spoke in a high-pitched lisp that grated on my nerves. Although he was my friend, I was constantly irritated by his wimpy, know-it-all manner-isms. He loved to raise his hand in class and answer all the teacher's questions.

Our teacher was an old lady named Mrs. Cline who had taught both my mother and Brian. She was a no-nonsense teacher from an earlier generation with white hair that she kept up in a bun. Her desk was in the front center of the room, and she sat there while we worked on our assignments. On this particular day, she rose from her desk and began writing out an assignment on the black-board. She was wearing a blue checkered dress that came down to her calves, and she wrote her letters out in neat swirling cursive. As she headed back to her desk and picked up a stack of papers, I studied the letters on the chalkboard, trying to decipher them.

"Suzie, will you please pass these out to the class?" Mrs. Cline asked.

A little girl in a pink jumper came forward and counted out the number of students in each row of desks. Then she gave the correct number of papers to the first row of students to pass along to the person behind them.

I looked down at the stapled papers passed to me. It was a story with questions at the end to answer as part of a report we were supposed to write. I immediately went into a quiet panic as I struggled with reading the first sentence on the page. The words made no sense. This would likely be another failing grade for me.

Donny raised his hand.

"Yes, Donny?" Mrs. Cline said.

"Teacher, can we earn extra credit if we write more than one page?" Donny asked in his high, whining voice.

Mrs. Cline laughed, obviously pleased by his question. "Well, if you want to write more than one page, you certainly may. But we'll have to see about the extra credit."

"What if we turn it in early?" he said.

At this point, I had had enough of Donny's know-it-all attitude and girly voice. I turned around and glared at him.

"What?" Donny met my gaze with a silly expression on his face.

Without a thought, I shot my fist out and socked him right in the nose. Donny screamed, covering his face as blood seeped between his fingers and down his chin. I stared at him, dumbfounded. *Why had I done that?* Mrs. Cline stood motionless at the blackboard, her hand raised as if to stop me from doing what I had already done. Donny's screeching cries echoed off the walls and ceiling. Before Mrs. Cline could say anything, I ran out of the classroom and down the long hallway to the school's large entrance door. My heart was pounding, and I stopped at the door for an instant to see if anyone was following. The hallway was empty. I pushed the heavy door open and ran a half block down the side street until I reached Broadway, a four-lane road that cut through blocks of retail stores and houses. We lived on Prince Street, almost half a mile away. It was around 10 a.m., and there was little traffic as I ran down Broadway, past Lincoln High School, and then turned onto Prince.

Mom was in the kitchen when I burst through the front door and ran into my room. Throwing myself on my bed, I sobbed face down into the mattress.

She followed me and knelt beside my bed.

"What happened, Wynn? Why are you home?" Mom rubbed my quivering shoulders until I finally calmed down and turned over. She handed me a tissue. "You need to tell me what happened."

I blew my nose and wiped my puffy eyes. Then I blurted out, "I hit Donny in the nose. I really socked him good."

Mom pulled back and looked at me. "Why would you do that?"

"I don't know," I said, starting to cry again. "He just made me so mad."

"Was it something he said or did to you?" she asked.

"No. He didn't do anything. I was just mad."

Mom nodded but didn't look satisfied. "Well, you're going to apologize. I'm taking you back right now."

I resisted. Couldn't it wait until tomorrow? But she said no, and she marched me the half-mile back to school and into the classroom.

The whole class was staring at me when we walked in. My head was bowed in disgrace, and my mother was determined to make things right. Donny was sitting at his desk, holding an ice pack against his nose. Several bloody tissues were scattered on the floor around him. After making me apologize to Mrs. Cline, Mom marched me up to Donny and made me apologize to him as well.

I was held in for recess that day and was sternly lectured to by Mrs. Cline. But the punishment had little effect. The very next day, I repeated the performance, socking poor Donny in the face and then running home. Again, my mom marched me back to school to apologize. Thankfully, Donny suffered no serious injuries from these assaults, and he and I became better friends. But I often wonder what caused me to hit him. Was it frustration over being unable to read? Pent-up anger over feeling helpless when I was raped? Rage over never being able to communicate what happened to me? Or did picking on a smaller boy help me feel empowered? Perhaps all of the above.

*Me and Brian (with two neighborhood friends)
in front of our house on Prince Street.*

Blowing bubbles in my favorite rocker. Age eight.

3

LOST AND FOUND

When I was ten years old, my family moved to a bigger house in Highland Park, a neighborhood in Los Angeles about five miles from Lincoln Heights. Our new house was an old wooden structure with a large cement porch and side stone pillars. I loved to sit on our canopy-covered porch swing in all kinds of weather—especially when rare summer storms would move in from over the mountains. Our house was built on a third of an acre with a huge backyard and a small orchard of fruit trees. Coming from a farming family, my dad was in his element there, planting a large garden and even raising chickens and rabbits. My mom loved it as well, canning all we grew over the summer, including pears, apples, and guavas.

Through my experience helping my dad with the animals, I learned the difference between animals that were pets and animals that were meant to eat. I had always wanted a dog, but my father had told me our previous house and yard were too small.

"A dog needs a big backyard," he would say. "If we

ever move to a place with a decent yard, I promise I'll get you a dog."

He made good on his promise a few weeks after we moved. My aunt Lura and uncle Ben, who raised award-winning German shepherds, came over with a housewarming present just for me—the cutest German shepherd puppy I had ever laid eyes on. The pup had a long brown snout, large pointed ears, and gangly long legs for her size; it was love at first sight for both me and her. She was probably worth five hundred dollars untrained, but I didn't know about that. All I knew was that I had a dog of my very own, and I was ecstatic. I named her Sierra and took her everywhere I could. She was my best friend.

But my elation soon turned to sadness one day when my father noticed the odd way she was walking. He raised the subject at the dinner table. I could tell there was something wrong by the tone of his voice.

"Wynn," he said gently, "have you noticed Sierra is limping?"

I shrugged my shoulders.

"I think we better take her back to Ben and Lura and see if there's something wrong with her. If there is, they'll know what to do."

I nodded, but I didn't really understand what he meant.

A few days later, we headed over to my aunt and uncle's house with me and Sierra sitting in the backseat of the car. Sierra was happy as ever, her head out the open window and her long tongue hanging sideways from her mouth.

My uncle's mood was somber as he watched Sierra limp around their living room. He advised us that he would take her to a veterinarian for a thorough examination and x-rays. When the report came back from the vet, the news wasn't good. Sierra had a rare hip disease, and the vet recommended we put her down.

"Put her down?" I said when my parents broke the news to me. "You mean *kill her*?" I was stunned. This wasn't like the chickens and rabbits we slaughtered for food. This was my best friend! I pleaded with them not to do it.

"I know it's hard, son. I know," my father said quietly. "But this isn't something that's going to go away. It'll get worse and worse until she's in so much pain she'll long to be put down. You don't want her to suffer like that, do you?"

He was right. I knew it in my head, but my heart told me otherwise. I got down on my knees with my dog's head between my hands and kissed her. Then I sobbed uncontrollably with my face in her thick fur.

Losing my best friend like this had a profound effect on me. It was the second real loss in my young life — the first being the loss of my innocence at age six. My usual outgoing, happy-go-lucky personality was transformed into a quiet, morose boy. For days, I moped around the house with nothing to say unless directly spoken to.

My mood change rattled my father. He had known the same kind of love for a dog when he was a boy and understood how hurt I was. After a few weeks, he told me to get in the car because we were going to pick out a new dog at the pound. I didn't really want another dog, but as I walked with my dad down rows and rows of cages filled with sad and hopeless-looking animals, I suddenly became a boy with a mission. I had been powerless to save Sierra, but I could save one of these poor dogs. My father examined each dog closely. Finally, his eyes lit on a young, female black Labrador retriever.

"This is the one," he said.

Her name was Deja, and she became one of the best dogs I've ever had. My father was very fond of Deja as well. She came already trained, and she loved to chase anything we threw for her—sticks, balls, Frisbees . . . it didn't matter. She had a half-acre to run and play on, and my dad left her care up to me. Now that I look back, I believe he saw Deja as a companion because Brian was already in college, and I had no other siblings. This time in my life was probably the closest I had ever felt to my father. He worked hard, both at his job as a warehouse superintendent and on the property where we lived. He loved growing things—and I admired him for that, spending endless hours with him in the twilight or on the weekends harvesting the fruits of our labor. I learned from him a love for the land and for growing things, a love I still carry with me today.

Dad and Mom in our Highland Park backyard.

Me at age seven horseback riding with my father.

4

THE BIG LIE

The move to Highland Park also meant a new school—
Bushnell Way Elementary. I had lots of friends at my old
school and wasn't excited about starting the fifth grade
without them. I didn't know a soul at Bushnell and had
no idea what I needed to do to make new friends. I tried to
figure out ways to join in conversations, but no one seemed
to notice me. For an extrovert, this was unbearable.

After a week of sitting alone in the cafeteria during
lunch, I decided it was time to do something bold, and I
sat at a picnic table with a group of boys from my class.
They were arguing over an episode of *The Lone Ranger* and
barely gave me a passing glance. Being an avid TV viewer,
I easily joined in and was relieved when they listened to
me and responded to what I was saying. But then I became
overconfident and decided to show off.

"Do you ever watch the *Mickey Mouse Club*?"[2] I asked.

---

2 *Mickey Mouse Club* is was a long-running American variety television show that began
in 1955, produced by Walt Disney Productions and televised by ABC, featuring a regular but
ever-changing cast of teenage performers, known as Mouseketeers.

"Sure," the boy sitting next to me said. "What about it?"

"My sister's one of the Mouseketeers," I said.

They looked skeptical.

"Which Mouseketeer?" a boy sitting across from me asked.

"Cheryl," I said, intentionally naming a lesser-known Mouseketeer so that my story would sound more believable.

The boy next to me laughed. "Then why don't we ever see her? She's around our age. Why isn't she at school?"

"Because she's my half-sister," I explained. "She has a different dad and lives with him and his wife. She goes to a private school."

More questions came, and with each question, more lies. Even so, they began to buy my story, and my celebrity status spread throughout the school. I became instantly popular. Students approached me from other classes and grade levels, wanting to know if I ever watched the episodes while they were being filmed. Had I ever tried to be a Mouseketeer myself? When was my sister coming to visit? Then the questioners started demanding proof. They wanted to see a photograph of me with Cheryl. They wanted autographs. They wanted to see Cheryl in person.

The lie was gaining a life of its own, and I was desperate not to be found out. At home, I found a pad of paper and started signing Cheryl's name on each slip. Then I passed the autographs out before class.

"I saw Cheryl, and she signed these for me," I said.

"So you saw her yesterday?" a girl with blond pigtails asked. "How did you get there?"

"In a helicopter," I said boldly. "She lets me use her helicopter whenever I come for a visit."

The class became eerily quiet, and then several of the students broke out into laughter. Apparently, my helicopter story was ridiculous enough to convince even my most ardent fans that I was a fraud. Suddenly, I went from being "the boy with a famous sister" to "the boy who lies," and all my hopes of having friends at Bushnell were lost.

This was the third major loss in my life, and it made me feel worthless. *What's wrong with me? Why do I do these things?* I didn't feel like I could come to my parents with these questions because we never talked about our personal struggles. Looking back now, I may have been more willing to open up to my parents if I had seen them talking about serious matters together. But they never did. Everything was always on the surface: How was work? How was your day? While they often spoke about religious matters, they never talked about personal things, and they never asked me personal questions. Mom counseled other women in our church, but she didn't do so in front of me. The idea of modeling this kind of communication was foreign to them, and their lack of communication hindered me from dealing with the struggles in my life.

⁓

This lonely existence went on for six months until three girls approached me in the playground while I was sitting on a swing, swaying back and forth.

"Hi, Wynn," a large-eyed brunette named Margo said. "We were wondering if you could answer a question."

I waited, grateful to have someone to talk to.

"Why'd you lie and tell that story?"

I sighed. The fact that they were asking was such a relief. But how could I explain? One thing was certain: I had to tell the truth.

"I was new here, and I didn't know how to make friends," I said. "I thought if I lied and told everyone that I knew someone famous, the other kids would want to be my friends. But I didn't realize it would totally ruin my life. I'll never have any friends now."

Margo nodded as she listened, then declared, "We'll be your friends. You can hang out with us."

It seemed too good to be true. These cute little girls meant what they said and became my friends. Little by little, I started regaining some self-confidence.

5

PUBERTY

The only music I knew while growing up were the hymns in church and show tunes from famous musicals. I enthusiastically sang the hymns loudly both in general worship and as a soloist in front of the congregation. Singing was the greatest joy in my young life. It helped me to feel valuable and close to God.

But something happened in 1957, when I was eleven years old, that almost stopped me from singing altogether. Puberty set in early, and the notes that always came out perfectly started croaking out in low and high decibels beyond my control.

Lincoln Heights Foursquare Church was a small adobe structure resembling a Spanish mission. There were about 130 people in our congregation, and we sat in connected wooden seats that folded up when we stood to worship. Our head pastor was a woman named Maybelle Cutting—a staunch holiness preacher trained up by Aimee Semple McPherson. She was in her mid-fifties and never missed an opportunity to warn the congregation about the wages of sin. I was terrified of her. Mildred Poole, the assistant pastor, was about fifteen years younger and much more to my liking because she was down to earth, compassionate, and full of fun.

I remember the day I realized my voice was no longer the high soprano that impressed the congregation when I sang solos. I was singing during worship in church as I had always done. But after the hymns were over and the congregation started milling about, saying hello to one another, Pastor Maybelle came down from the platform and approached me.

"Hello, Wynn. How are you today?" she said, standing over me and shaking my hand. Although she was smiling, her face was serious.

I smiled back and told her I was fine. But then I wondered why she didn't move on to say hello to someone else. She dropped my hand and drew nearer to speak. "I was wondering, Wynn," she said, pausing. "Could you sing a little softer? You're having trouble keeping the notes, and it's starting to distract our worship."

I was shocked. No one had ever complained about my voice before. I was the kid with the pitch-perfect voice. Everyone knew that. *I sound terrible? How can that be?* I rushed out of the sanctuary and into the bathroom. Slamming the door of the stall, I sat down on the toilet and wept. *How can God do this to me? How can He take away the one thing I love the most?*

Because puberty had temporarily ruined my singing

voice, I asked my parents if I could learn to play the violin. I still had a love for music that needed an outlet. I was drawn to the violin after seeing someone playing it in the movie *Intermezzo* on TV. For some reason, the haunting song played by the violinist in that movie mesmerized me. My mom and dad thought it was a good idea and encouraged me to talk to the orchestra teacher at Bushnell. Most of the students who learned to play the violin started in the second grade, so the teacher had her doubts about me starting in the fifth grade. But she gave me a chance, and I learned to play as well as most of the other students in only a few months. My parents were so impressed at my progress that they hired a violin teacher to come in once a week for private lessons.

Playing violin during this time in my life helped me to fill in the hours after school when I would normally be out playing with friends. I also had Deja, my parents, and television.

6

MOLESTATION

By the summer of my eleventh year, I was already sexually mature. I was tall for my age—five-foot-four—and my voice was low and masculine. Even so, I was still very much a boy, with little understanding of what was happening to my body.

My parents were heavily involved in church and openly practiced the gift of hospitality with everyone they knew. It seemed like we always had visitors at our house, including friends from church and visiting missionaries.

Many of these visitors were young women who gravitated to my mom because she helped them navigate tough situations and encouraged them to grow closer to God. Mom had a way of speaking wisdom into their lives that inspired them to deepen their spiritual journeys. Pat was one of the women who was mentored by my mom. A heavyset woman in her mid-twenties, Pat had a cool air of confidence about her and always wore red lipstick. She was a single mother with a five-year-old boy, and she often came to our house to visit while he was away visiting his grandma. After a while, I noticed something odd about Pat's behavior. Although she came to visit my mom, she started giving me more attention. She complimented me when saying hello, and then she started talking to me one on one. Eventually, she began asking me to join her and my mother while she visited. Because I was only eleven and had few friends my age, this made me feel very grown up.

I had no idea what her true intentions were, and neither did my parents. But it all became clear one hot summer day.

It was warmer than normal, even for mid-July. Although air conditioning was becoming popular in the 1950s, there was still no central air conditioning in households, and our house didn't even have a window unit. Instead, we relied on fans to keep things bearable. Pat and I were sitting on the couch as Mom busied herself in the kitchen fixing dinner. The large fan in our living room groaned as it circulated hot air around the room. I was shirtless, wearing only a pair of jean cutoffs, and felt listless while listening to Pat complain.

"I hope we get some relief soon," she said loudly so that my mom could hear her from the kitchen. "This heat is unbearable."

Suddenly remembering, I jumped up from the couch to get one of my mom's little handheld fans that sprayed mist.

When I returned, Pat was holding a plastic bottle. "Have you been wearing suntan lotion, Wynn? It looks like you're getting too much sun."

I shook my head.

"Do you want me to put some of this on your back? It'll help you to tan instead of burn."

"Okay," I said, turning my back to her.

The smell of coconut oil filled the room as she slowly rubbed the lotion into the skin below my shoulders. It felt a little awkward, but I didn't say anything. Once she covered my back, she asked me to turn around and started rubbing the lotion on my thigh. This made me even more uncomfortable. *Why is she doing this? I'm perfectly capable of putting lotion on my leg,* I thought.

My mother's voice grew louder from the kitchen, and Pat jerked her hand away just before my mom appeared in the doorway. I looked at Pat, who had an odd smile on her face. She talked casually with my mom for a while, her voice even and calm.

"I have so many things to fix around my apartment," Pat said, "but it's hard to get anything done when I'm so busy."

"Oh, dear, why didn't you say something earlier?" my mom said. "I'm sure Hal and I can come over on a Saturday to help you. What do you need done?"

Pat waved her hand, dismissing the thought. "Oh, I couldn't," she said. "You two are so busy with your own family. It's just little things that I could use an extra hand with . . ." Then, as if a bright idea suddenly came to her, she said, "Would it be okay if I borrowed Wynn to help me with something today?"

My mom was smiling and nodding her head. "Of course," she said. "Wynn, you wouldn't mind helping Pat, would you?"

I shrugged. "I guess not."

The next thing I knew, Pat was driving me across town to her bungalow. As we walked into her living room, she motioned for me to sit on the couch.

"I'll be right back," she said.

After several minutes, she stood in the doorway of her bedroom wearing only a bra and panties. "Why don't you come in here, Wynn, and put some lotion on me?"

I looked around the room and then back at her. "Okay," I said.

She led me into her bedroom, and there she seduced me into having sex with her. I didn't understand where those urges came from. My parents had never talked to me about hormones or puberty, so I was completely unprepared. My only thought at the moment was that this was the best feeling I'd ever had.

While this was happening, I later learned of a related scene playing out between my mother and her friend Sandi. Sandi was an intercessory prayer warrior[3] in our church and had been praying that same hour when the Holy Spirit spoke to her about what Pat was doing to me. This prompted Sandi to immediately call my mom and ask her where I was.

"He's over at Pat's helping her with some chores," my mom said. "Why?"

"Oh, no," Sandi said. "We've got to stop her!" Then she told my mother what the Holy Spirit had spoken to her. "She's up to no good."

My mom hung up the phone and frantically called my

---

3 A person who is gifted by God to pray regularly for people as led by the Holy Spirit.

dad, who drove home to pick her up. Then they headed across town to Pat's house.

Sandi, who lived closer to Pat, arrived at the bungalow first and rapped sharply on the front door. Pat jumped out of bed and rapidly put on her robe. She pushed me into her closet, throwing my clothes in after me, and whispered, "Don't say anything; be quiet."

I didn't know what to think. One minute I was on top of the world and the next I was trembling with fear in the closet. I leaned my ear against the door and heard Sandi's muffled voice. "Where is he? I know what you're doing. You should be ashamed!"

Pat denied everything and eventually managed to close the door on Sandi without letting her into the house. She waited until Sandi had driven away, and then she ordered me to get dressed and drove me home. As I watched the scenery whiz by, I tried to sort things out in my thoughts.

"Everything's fine," Pat said. "I just need to get you home."

I didn't respond, and my silence only seemed to make things more uncomfortable. I sensed that something terrible had happened, but I didn't understand the ramifications. Pat was driving too fast; her cool demeanor had disappeared.

When we arrived at my house, Grandma Arissa was the only one home. She coldly glared at me as Pat and I walked in. "What have you done?" she asked me. Her voice had an edge to it, a tone she had never used with me before.

"I haven't done anything, Grandma," I said. "I was helping Pat."

My grandmother shook her head and turned to Pat. "I think you'd better leave," she said in a stern voice.

Pat gladly complied.

When my parents came home, my mom was crying. My father stood silent, withdrawn. I was confused. Both seemed incapable of knowing what to do. I needed them to put their arms around me, tell me everything was all right and that they loved me. Instead, they seemed lost.

"We need to pray for forgiveness," my father finally said in a weak voice.

I was dumbfounded. *Forgiveness for what?*

Following my father's wishes, the three of us knelt and prayed. But my heart wasn't in it. All I could think about was the look of disgust on my father's face, and I felt an overwhelming sense of shame. *He blames me for this,* I thought.

I felt abandoned and rejected by him, and it would take a very long time for me to recognize the implications this feeling would have on my life.[4] Because we never talked about it, I formed assumptions—primarily that my father was ashamed of me and that sex with women was bad. The sexual urges within me raged on with more intensity than ever, and although I'm sure puberty played a part in this, I also believe the shame and trauma from my youth had morphed and twisted my urges into something unnatural and unholy.

---

4 See Appendix for information on how the lack of open communication in families can lead to problems in identity in children.

I only know this now as an adult looking back. As a boy, I was a clueless pawn being pushed about by a brewing turmoil of desire mixed with shame and secrecy. By the time I was thirteen, I was ready to give in to any temptation that came my way.

Whatever closeness I had felt toward my father before the events of this day had now evaporated. In its place was a chasm that I was unwilling and unable to cross.

7

DARKNESS CLOSING IN

I've always enjoyed being outdoors, and I often walked through the parks that lined the old Pasadena Freeway near where I lived. It was during one of these walks when I fell prey to a trap the enemy had set.[5] I was thirteen years old and decided to stop at the public restroom to use the toilet. The inside was mostly cement and dark, lit only by sunlight that came through slatted openings near the ceiling. The three wide stalls were completely open with no doors. I didn't pay any mind to the middle-aged man who followed me in, but after I flushed the toilet, he was standing in front of me.

"I have a question for you," he said in a polite voice. "How would you like me to do something with you to make you feel good?"

I had no idea what he was talking about, but I pretended I did.

"Okay," I said.

---

5   "The enemy" is another name used for Satan. Satan knows where we are weakest and how to tempt us into sin through those weaknesses.

I'm not sure why I didn't run away—only that something was enticing in the way he came on to me.

The next thing I knew, this man was touching me. It was very scary, but there was also a strong force within me that liked the feeling and the attention. As odd as this may seem, I believe the disconnect from my father fueled this desire because I was trying to fill that fatherless void in my life.

I was both energized and traumatized over the experience and said nothing about it to anyone. Instead, I added it to my growing list of sexual encounters. As the following weeks passed, I couldn't get this latest experience out of my head, and I returned to the same toilet several times looking for the man in hopes of having the same experience again. I was hooked on the excitement and adrenaline rush.

About the third time I returned to the restroom, I ran into two men having sex at the urinal. One of the men was middle-aged, while the other looked to be around nineteen. Startled, I left the bathroom and watched the door from behind a tree. When the older man left, I walked back in. The younger man, who looked like a surfer with tanned skin and sun-bleached hair, was in one of the stalls, and I went into the adjacent stall to watch him through a large hole. I found myself very attracted to him. The sight of his naked body did something inside me that became a driving force, pushing me to walk right up and boldly proposition him.

He gladly obliged, and this experience with a young man imprinted itself into my mind in a way that twisted my thought process. I was never quite the same afterward and could think of little else. I returned to the same public restroom, over and over, trying to find him to repeat the experience. But I never saw him again.

⁓

Most of the time, the restroom was empty when I ventured in. But one day in 1959, when I was thirteen, a middle-aged man was standing next to the urinal, sizing me up like he was interested. Emboldened by my previous experiences, I strolled over and propositioned him for sex.

His response was not what I expected.

"Come with me," he said, spinning me around and pushing me out into the sunlight. My heart was racing with fear. I thought about running away, but he seemed to know what I was thinking and grabbed my wrist.

Another man who had been watching through vent slats from a crawlspace behind the wall followed us out. "Nice work," he said, laughing and shaking his head. "I swear they seem to get younger every year."

The men were undercover police detectives, staking out the restroom to catch men who were propositioning others for sex. They handcuffed me and then shoved me into their unmarked police car. I was terrified. All I knew about sex was that it wasn't talked about and therefore had to be kept secret. I didn't know what homosexuality was and that it was against the law to have sex in a public place. The possibility of getting arrested for this never even entered my mind. I fell over and curled into a fetal position in the backseat.

"Do you hear that?" one of the detectives said. "The little perv is crying. Poor little guy. You should go back there and comfort him."

"Shut up," the other man said.

I wasn't sure if he was talking to me or to his partner, but I tried my best to stifle my cries.

I was still shaking when we arrived at the Highland Park City Jail, a large historic brick building with two stories and a basement. The officers led me through the booking process and then sat me down at one of their desks and called my parents. How was I going to explain this to my mom and dad? I waited for almost an hour until a police officer led me into a large, sparsely populated waiting room. My parents were sitting on a wooden bench, looking pale and exhausted. My dad stood up slowly as I walked over, and my mom stayed sitting and looked at me with sad red eyes. We silently walked out to the car.

It wasn't until we were driving home that my mom turned around to face me in the backseat. "What happened, Wynn? I need to understand."

I shrugged and shook my head. "I don't know," I mumbled.

My father didn't say anything, but I could tell he was listening.

"Were you hurt?" she asked.

"No."

"What did you do?" she said.

I shrugged again. "Nothing. I just talked to some guy."

"But they arrested you. Why did they arrest you? You need to—"

"Marionne," my father interrupted, holding up his hand to silence her. "We'll talk about this later."

But we never did. It was almost as if my parents were hoping it would all go away if we avoided the subject.

~~

Because I was a minor, my parents had to join me in court when I was summoned. I was assigned a pasty-face public defender who barely spoke to me. He told the judge that, as a first-time offender and juvenile, I promised never to do anything of this sort again. My parents also pledged to supervise my comings and goings more closely. They sat with me on a bench, my father on my left and my mother on my right, both looking straight ahead and answering the judge in quiet tones. I was so humiliated I could barely whisper when the judge addressed me.

"Stand up, son," he ordered.

I stood, my legs feeling like rubber bands. I kept my head bowed as the judge spoke.

"Since this is the first time you've ever been in trouble with the law, I'm going to drop the charges," he said. "But I need your word that this funny business won't happen again. Do you understand?"

I nodded.

"Look at me, boy."

I looked up. The judge, a large man with a full head of white hair, peered down at me, his reading glasses resting on the edge of his nose. "I'm very serious," he said. "If I ever see you in my courtroom again, I will not be so kind."

As I looked into his iron gaze, I knew he meant it.

"Yes, sir," I said.

8

HELP OR HINDRANCE?

My parents never spoke to me about the arrest nor my behavior that caused it. Just like sweeping a pile of dirt under a rug, it was hidden from view. But the dirt was still there, along with the shame.

This cover-up only encouraged me to continue leading a double life. On the one hand, I was a boy who took on leadership roles in the youth group at my church and played violin at school, even earning the first chair before graduating from junior high.

I suppose my parents took heart in these achievements, feeling confident that the dark side of me—the dirt under the rug—was truly gone. But keeping silent only empowered the shame and unholy passions, driving me even deeper into my degradation. I still longed for the attention and the thrill of that hidden obsession, and I found myself thinking about ways to slink off to the park and look for the surfer and the experience I longed to replicate with him. You'd think the shock and disgrace of being arrested would have been a deterrent for me to quit the behavior—

or at least to not return to the same park restroom. But no. The longings grew stronger, and I started venturing back, hoping to find the surfer. Although he never reappeared, I did connect with other guys and became quite adept at approaching grown men for sex—even at the tender age of fourteen.

It didn't take long before I approached the wrong man again and found myself facing a second offense. Heading behind bars once more, I'll never forget how one officer—a woman about my mother's age—made me feel as she booked me into jail. She was sitting behind a metal desk and told me to look her in the eye when she was speaking to me.

"Just so you know," she said, her icy tone slicing through me like a steel blade, "I have three sons, and I would never, *never* allow you to play with them or even be in the same room with them."

I was mortified, wishing I could dissolve into the floor.

My second arrest didn't help to improve communication with my parents either. Instead, the unspoken heaviness became worse. Once again, we were entombed in silence while driving home, except for the occasional sighs from my mom. The shame I felt was suffocating, and there was an empty ache in my stomach like someone had gut-punched me. Apparently, what I had done was too horrific for words or even for punishment. Although I was in denial about my behavior and defended my innocence to all who tried to accuse me, I still needed something from them—some kind of consequence. Even a harsh word from my father would have been better than his silence. It was as if nothing would suffice to take away my shame. I needed my parents to explain to me why this behavior was bad for me, but they were too stunned and ashamed to communicate with me in a meaningful way. So they avoided the subject.

A week later, I was once again sitting in the courtroom between my parents, relieved to see a different judge peering down at me. This man was younger than the judge who ruled over my previous arrest, and he spoke in soft tones. Because this was my second offense, he said he could not drop the charges. However, he would sentence me to several months of counseling instead of juvenile hall. My parents would need to find the appropriate counselor and report back to the court.

As we pulled into our driveway afterward, my father turned the car's engine off and sat facing forward. When he finally spoke, his voice sounded hollow and weak. "I guess we'll need to find you some help with this," he said.

I had no idea what this meant, but I was relieved that I wouldn't be going to juvenile hall.

~

The counselor they found charged fifty dollars per hour—an enormous sum in 1960. He was a chunky middle-aged man with wire-rimmed glasses and large ears. Except for his framed degrees and certificates, there were no decorations on the drab walls. The floor was cold linoleum, and his office felt more like a mental ward than a safe environment for bearing one's soul. He didn't look at me as I walked in, and he made no move to introduce himself or even shake my hand. His eyes were fixed on a stack of papers in front of him as he sat behind his desk, and he motioned for me to sit as if he were swatting away a fly. I watched as he methodically read through the paperwork, licking his fingers before turning each page. Every so often, he would ask me a question.

"You have an older brother?"

"Yes."

"How is your relationship with him?"

"Fine."

Then he'd scribble something down.

"Does he live at home?"

"No."

"Why?"

"He's twenty-four and in the army."

"I see." More scribbling.

"How about your parents? How is your relationship with them?"

"Fine."

"No fights?"

"No."

"Hmmm . . . "

And so it went. I don't recall him ever asking me anything about my arrest or about any traumatic events that could have caused my behavior. But even if he had, I would never have opened up to him.

I don't think my parents ever bought into the idea of therapy either. Although they were faithful in taking me and paying the cost, they had decided on a different course of action. I didn't discover what this was until one day after school when my mother announced we were going to church. My father was at work, and it seemed like an odd time for a service, but I followed her to the car.

As we pulled into the near-empty parking lot, I felt a chill run through me. Pastor Maybelle Cutting was waiting for us inside, along with seven other women. The assistant pastor, Sister Mildred Poole, was not present, and I missed her. Unlike Sister Maybelle, Mildred had always been kind to me. But she was not there, and the nine women in the room—including my mother—seemed bent on a course of action I was not privy to until Pastor Cutting asked the women to surround me.

"We're going to cast out these demons of homosexuality and perversion," she announced.

I was shocked. Suddenly the spotlight was on me but not in a way that I had ever craved. They began to pray, quietly at first but then louder and louder, denouncing the devil and ordering the spirits of homosexuality and perversion to flee. I was overwhelmed, falling to my knees and crumpling to the floor in uncontrollable shaking. Eventually, they stopped praying, and Pastor Cutting announced that the demons were gone. She seemed exhilarated and satisfied.

My mother looked both relieved and concerned. But I didn't feel free. Undoubtedly something had occurred in my spirit, but it wasn't peaceful or calming. And my desire for deviant behavior didn't cease. Instead, the deep fear and mistrust of women that had started with my molestation and increased with the woman police officer only became stronger. Without realizing it, these wounds evolved into taking offense against women and God. It was only a matter of time before this offense would become resentment, then bitterness, then anger, and eventually rebellion and hatred.

A few weeks later, I was back to my old behaviors, only now I was more careful, cunning, and secretive. I became a confident two-faced liar. My sexual addiction drove me to find ingenious ways of seducing others—even heterosexual guys. I took my time, grooming them until they were ready and willing to have sex with me. It seemed nothing could stand in my way.

9

POSITIVE INFLUENCES

Leading a double life wasn't easy. Constantly aware that at any moment I would be found out and exposed for who I really was, I was a quagmire of stress, turmoil, and shame. Even so, I became hooked on the danger—the adrenaline rush I felt every time I acted on my wicked pursuits. It became a provocative addiction, ever driving me forward.

My secret passions became my new god as I pretended to be a good Christian while indulging in ungodly pleasures. Even so, God had a way of keeping His hand on me.

Although I deeply mistrusted most women, there remained two women in my life who never gave up on me and who quietly worked behind the scenes, sowing seeds of decency, kindness, and goodness.

The first of these was my mother. While the rift between me and my father felt like a chasm beyond repair, my relationship with my mom was my anchor; I knew that she would love me no matter what I did. We had a deep bond not only because she was my mother but also because we were so alike. She understood my love for music because she was a musician. She encouraged me to start singing again after puberty, and she helped me to realize that, although different from the high soprano voice I had as a boy, my voice was now a smooth baritone.

The other positive female influence in my life was Sister Mildred Poole. She was a playful woman in her late thirties who loved spending time with children and teenagers. Her presence as the assistant pastor of our church and her words in the pulpit served as balm to the wounds often inflicted by Pastor Maybelle's fire-and-brimstone style of preaching. Mildred taught about the love of God in a patient and soothing voice, and she seemed to sympathize and understand sinners instead of condemning them. Although opposites, Maybelle and Mildred worked well together because they balanced each other out, between having a healthy fear of God and knowing the love of God. If Mildred disapproved of Maybelle's tactics, she never let on. She had a deep respect for Maybelle.

I've often wondered if Mildred's absence during my exorcism had been purposeful, but I never asked her because I knew that would put her in an uncomfortable position. She would never say anything negative about Maybelle. However, when Mildred approached me a few days after the event and asked if I'd like to go deep-sea fishing with her, I suspect it was her way of reaching out to a traumatized boy. Mildred went deep-sea fishing almost every Saturday, but she had never asked me to join her before.

~~~

It was still dark when Mildred picked me up at 4 a.m. in her small Mini Cooper. I almost didn't recognize her because she was wearing coveralls and a faded baseball cap—so different from the long, conservative dresses she wore in church. When we arrived at the coastline, the sky was just beginning to lighten along the horizon behind us, and the cool ocean breezes invigorated me. I breathed in the faint smell of salted seaweed as I followed Mildred down a wooden dock, carrying her tackle box and fishing pole.

The *Sadie Blue* was a small fishing vessel weathered by years of use but well equipped with bait, fishing equipment, and even a small galley kitchen. Mildred was on a first-name basis with the boat crew and warmly greeted them, joking with the captain, an older man with whiskered cheeks, about the strapping young man she had hired to carry her gear. I was beaming and couldn't wait to get started.

"I'll show him how it's done, Mike," she reassured the captain.

"Yes." He winked and handed me a large fishing pole. "Just make sure he sends the chum into the water and not on the deck."

Mildred chuckled and patted me on the back. "We won't have to worry about this one. I have a feeling he's a true seaman."

And she was right. While rookie fishermen around the boat were vomiting their breakfasts into the sea, I never had even a hint of seasickness. The skies were clear and the sea calm, its rolling swell lulling the boat into a comfortable rhythm. My first catch, a large sea bass, was so heavy and strong I almost dropped my pole.

"Hold tight!" Mildred said, her voice an excited pitch.

After pulling and reeling until my arms and hands ached, I heaved the fish out of the water and into Mildred's waiting net. The fish was huge—a real beauty!

"That's the way," she said, spilling the fish onto the deck and then slamming a hammer to its head to still its flopping body.

"You're a natural," she said, smiling at the catch. "You hungry?"

I was famished. My arms, hands, and shoulders ached, but it felt good. She handed me some money and told me to get some grub. I must have eaten three large hamburgers that day, the work and the salty air fueling my hunger. I can't remember food ever tasting so delicious.

Mildred and I went fishing together several times over the next few years, and we became close friends. We both loved catching yellowfin tuna, and I remember the first time I caught a thirty-pounder. It was the most exhilarating experience I've ever had on the ocean.

Mildred never asked about my sexual struggles, but she seemed to understand and made a point to love me through them.

Although these positive influences and experiences didn't change my course, I believe they did sow seeds of goodness in my heart. I wasn't consciously aware of them, but God knew what He was doing.

Pastor Mildred Poole (R) with her friends Janet and Claudia on one of our fishing trips.

At fourteen, holding up a tiny snowman at Yellowstone National Park while on a family holiday.

10

THE DARKER SIDE

When I was still in junior high school, I set my eye on a young man in our church youth group who was six years older. He had graduated from high school and was not homosexual, but that did not stop me.

I clearly remember the first time I really *saw* Justin. Without thinking, my passion rose to a raging force. He was handsome and muscular, with a straightforward yet innocent demeanor. He was different than any of the other males in my life and seemed to encapsulate everything I wanted to be. In a way, he reminded me of the surfer, my first real passionate attraction. I spent hours scheming how I could get close to him and became fixated. For months, I groomed him like a lioness seeking its prey. Unnoticed, I stalked him and planned, not bringing any attention to myself and my obvious goal of devouring him.[6]

---

6   Leanne Payne, in her book *Crisis in Masculinity*, calls this the cannibalistic compulsion. Payne was a Christian pastoral counselor and a prominent authority on treating homosexual men and women, even though her methods were not always what clients expected. In counseling sessions, Payne displayed a knack for asking unorthodox questions, such as: "Do you know why cannibals eat people? Cannibals eat only those they admire, and they eat them to get their traits" (*Crisis in Masculinity* 28).

How can I get close to him so he'll accept me? I wondered.

I had heard he liked playing basketball at the high school gym on the weekends when it was open to the public. Although I had no interest in basketball, I decided this was my best opportunity. After our youth group meeting at the church, he was standing with a group of girls when I approached him.

"I heard you like to play basketball," I said.

That got his attention. "Do you play?" he asked.

"I wish. I don't know how."

"Really? You've never played?"

"No, but I'd love to learn."

"Well, I can teach you. But it would have to be on a Saturday because I work during the week."

"That'd be great. I'll ask my parents."

I asked him for his phone number, and he gladly scribbled it down on a piece of scrap paper.

I was in.

My parents knew Justin and thought he would be a good role model. As I walked into the gym after they dropped me off, squeaking sneakers and the hammering sounds of basketballs ricocheted in all directions, while athletic guys ran up and down the court. I was nervous and looked for Justin among the players. He was wearing shorts that came just above his knees and showed off his muscular legs—by far the best-looking guy in the gym and one of the better players. I could feel my heart pounding in expectation.

After the makeshift game was over, the gym emptied as most of the other players left for the showers. Justin smiled as I approached him. We talked, and he began instructing me on the correct form to use in shooting baskets. He lined me up a short distance from the hoop and demonstrated his shooting technique. Then he watched as I tried to duplicate what he showed me.

My first shot fell short of the hoop. I slumped my shoulders and shook my head.

"Don't worry. Just take another shot," he said, passing me the ball. "Everyone does that the first time they try."

I shot again. This time the ball hit the rim.

"Good! Now put a little more strength into it."

I did what he said, and the ball flew over the rim and hit the backboard.

"Now hold off just a little," he said.

He encouraged and instructed me over and over until I finally made a basket.

"That's it!" he said. "See? Practice makes perfect. It takes a lot of practice."

I loved his caring attitude and sensed I could use it to my advantage.

"Is it okay if I come here every Saturday so that you can help me get better?" I asked.

"Sure," he said. "I can let you know at youth group if I can make it the following Saturday."

When we were finished, we headed to the showers. Justin began stripping down in front of me, and my heart raced. He was about six feet tall, and his body was chiseled with developed chest muscles and biceps.

I was undressing at the same time, and although I was a little chubby and short, my desire for him was so strong that I didn't feel self-conscious.

We chatted as we showered. "I hope you don't mind me asking," I said, "but did it take long to look like you do now?"

Proudly, he told me that he had been a skinny kid. "I always wanted to have muscles," he said. "So I started working on it. It took a few years to get to this."

"That's what I want too," I said.

Justin nodded and agreed to help me. From that moment, I put all my efforts into getting as close as possible to him. I craved to be like him and to be with him because of my sense of inadequacy and loneliness. In short, I was infatuated, and it seemed right.

Over time, he began treating me like a little brother. I opened up to him about my struggles with being accepted by my peers and having confidence, which endeared me to him. I became his project. In his eyes, he was mentoring me to become a healthy, self-confident young man. I created a safe place for him to talk, just between me and him. He wanted to help me in any way he could, and I used that to con him into thinking he was helping me by having sex with me. Eventually, I was able to seduce him.

Understandably, this young man was so ashamed that he never told a soul. Shortly after, he left the church and never spoke to me again. I can only wonder what became of him. But that was my life—I would leave the carnage of my passions behind without much thought, moving on to my next victim in the wake of my last conquest's shame and dejection.

I realized early there was an enormous benefit to seducing guys instead of girls; I didn't have to worry about getting anyone pregnant, and the shame associated with homosexuality was so great that I knew my victims would keep quiet. It's not that I wasn't attracted to females; I had typical high-school crushes on girls. But I considered them off limits when it came to satisfying my sexual appetite.

By the time I started high school, I had already had numerous homosexual encounters. I was an addict, and my drug of choice was sex. Everything revolved around this craving—even my passion for music and sports.

Still, underneath my outward appearance of confidence and friendliness, I was a scared and insecure boy who thought he was ugly and worthless. I saw in other boys what I wanted in myself: good looks and masculinity. To this end, I pursued everything and anything that would put me around them. This is the reason I participated in sports during high school—so that I could be around masculine boys in the locker room. It's also why I joined the marching band. All of these activities gave me opportunities to make friends and grow close to other boys. Unbeknownst to them, I was a predator, craving to devour in them what I didn't feel I had in myself.

I didn't realize this at the time. I just wanted to get close enough to them so that I could wear them down and convince them that they would enjoy having sex with me. And my powers of persuasion were very convincing. Except for my past lovers, no one suspected what I was up to because I didn't act effeminate or flirtatious. I was just one of the guys.

Then I became overconfident and pursued the wrong boy.

It was during my freshman year of high school, and the boy was in the marching band with me. Although I knew he had no interest in doing anything sexual, I was so attracted to him I did everything in my power to win him over. The band conductor suggested I learn to play the oboe, and I asked this boy to help me. He agreed, and we started spending time together. One day when we were alone and practicing in the basement of the band room auditorium, I made my move. At first, he resisted my advances, but I wore him down, telling him it was perfectly safe. We could hide behind the props and instrument stands. Even if someone comes down, they'll never see us, I told him.

He finally gave in. Afterward, he was so ashamed he wouldn't look at me. I had his phone number and tried to connect with him several times, but he wouldn't take my calls. It became so uncomfortable I eventually dropped out of band and transferred to choir.

But that wasn't the end of it. The shame he felt was so obvious that his parents noticed it and managed to pry the story out of him several weeks later. Horrified, they contacted the school, and the school administration called the police.

I was sitting in one of my classes when the principal and two other men came in. The principal didn't say anything to the teacher but spoke directly to the class. "Wynn Thompson?"

I raised my hand.

"You need to come with us. Now."

Nervous and scared, I walked out of the classroom between the two men as the principal stood outside the door talking with the teacher. A feeling of doom descended over me, and I knew I was caught. I didn't say anything as we walked into the principal's office.

After closing the door, the principal leaned against his desk and motioned to the other men in the room. "These men are from the Highland Park Police Department. We received a complaint that you had sex with another boy on campus in the basement of the band auditorium. Is this true?"

What could I say? In my shame, my lying tongue fell silent. Suddenly, I felt like I was facing the woman detective again, her words ringing through my head: "I would *never* trust you to be around my sons, let alone play with them."

I tried to hold it in, to stand there and confess like a man. But my shoulders started to convulse uncontrollably until I broke down in sloppy, messy sobs.

Once again, I found myself riding in the back of a police car. I was frightened, but I didn't understand why they thought I had done something wrong. By this time, my conscience was seared. I figured that because I felt this attraction, it was normal to act on it. I had no inclination that it was tied to my past—being raped, molested, or the break I falsely perceived with my father. Perhaps if I had had some quality counseling or someone to talk to about it, I would have seen the connection. But I had no one. I was acting on feelings, and that seemed perfectly right to me.

I was taken into custody, and my parents were called. Oddly enough, the school didn't press charges. Nor did the parents of the boy. No surprise there. I'm sure both parties were not interested in having this incident made public.

My punishment? I was expelled from high school.

At seventeen, with my brother (L) and parents in front of our little pentecostal church.

11

A NEW PASSION

Things were gloomy and strained at home after my arrest and expulsion from high school. My parents must have realized their son was living a lie and had no intention of changing. But, really, I don't know what they were thinking because we never spoke about it. There was an unspoken no-talk rule in our home. They seemed bewildered, and a heaviness settled in. There was no yelling, no lectures, no further attempts to expel the demons. It was as if they had resigned themselves to the sad reality that there was nothing more they could do.

I didn't realize our lack of communication was creating a deep-seated shame within me. A part of me was relieved we never spoke about it. The last thing I wanted to do was address my addiction head on with my parents. And, frankly, I didn't want to give it up. Sexual perversion was becoming my identity and seemed to satisfy my deepest feelings of insecurity.

From the beginning of my abuses, no one ever really talked to me or asked what was going on. Thinking back,

I might have said something if I had been asked. But the question never came. Later, when the guilt and shame overtook me in my teens, I never wanted to add on more shame by telling anyone anything that I was doing. I had a false sense of security in my silence and didn't know it. It was the birth of true delusion.

Knowing I couldn't be trusted, my father had me on a tight leash. Rules surrounding my comings and goings were strictly enforced—mostly to protect the family from further embarrassment. I wasn't allowed to have friends over, and I was expected to finish my schooling through correspondence courses at home. By then, I was fifteen years old and craved attention from anyone who would listen. But this conflicted with my new situation. My mom tried her best to encourage me to keep up with my grade level, but the work piled up, and my dyslexia only exacerbated the problem. I never completed the units I needed to move on to the next grade level, which added to my disgrace.

My parents began looking for another option—a school that I could attend in person. This proved to be no easy task, and for a year I languished at home, feeling bored and isolated. Except for my dog, church activities, and phone calls with friends, my life felt like it was collapsing in on itself. Oddly enough, I never thought about suicide like others I knew growing up. Instead, I channeled my negative feelings and thoughts into a wall of protection around myself that I felt I could control.

My father had always been strict about keeping his sons away from activities he deemed "worldly," so movies, dancing, and most entertainment were out of the question anyway. How ironic this seems now! There I was, a boy sheltered from entertainment yet exposed to the vilest sexual sins of molestation, seduction, and perversion since the age of six. Yet I cannot blame my parents; they had no idea the extent of what had happened to me.

My father did allow a few exceptions to his strict entertainment rules: television and a small transistor radio that he had given to my brother. Television programming was a lot more family-friendly back in the 1950s and early '60s, and rock 'n' roll music was still in its early stages. When Brian joined the military, he gave me his radio. This device proved to not only be my escape from isolation but also a tool that rekindled my passion for music.

I vividly remember the day I first listened to it. It was tuned to KFWB, a popular Los Angeles rock station. At first, there was only the sound of the disc jockey's voice. Then a song started playing: "Silver Threads and Golden Needles" by the Springfields.[7] As I listened to the folk-rock guitar chords and harmonies, I was transfixed. I know it sounds crazy, but I had never heard rock 'n' roll music before, and it sent my pulse racing. I probably would have played that song over and over all day long if I had owned

---

7   A British pop-folk vocal trio who had success in the early 1960s in the United Kingdom, United States, and Ireland. They included singer Dusty Springfield and her brother, record producer Tom Springfield, along with Tim Feild, who was replaced by Mike Hurst.

the record. But as soon as it ended, another song began: "Breaking Up Is Hard to Do" by Neil Sedaka. My feet were tapping, my fingers drumming, and I was hooked! I suddenly knew what I wanted to do with the rest of my life—sing rock 'n' roll music!

⸻

While in choir at my high school, I met identical twin sisters who were professional singers and had a contract with Liberty Records.[8] They called themselves the Stansauk Sisters, and they had a manager named Jesse Hodges to help them. Although they were seniors when I was only a sophomore, we became good friends. Once my passion for singing was rekindled, I began practicing the songs from the radio until I knew a few by heart. Then I called the twins and sang the songs to them in mock auditions. Elated, the girls encouraged me to keep practicing, suggesting that I look in the newspaper for recording auditions. Every morning, I would wait for my father to leave for work and then sit at the kitchen table with the newspaper laid out in front of me, poring over the ad section. My mom would look over my shoulder, pointing out different possibilities and discussing my options. She was probably hoping this new passion would take the place of my past preoccupations.

Mom's enthusiastic support served as a counterbalance to my dad's religious adherence against anything

---

8   Liberty Records was a record label started in the United States by chairman Simon Waronker in 1955 with Al Bennett as president and Theodore Keep as chief engineer. It was reactivated in 2001 in the United Kingdom and had two previous revivals.

"Hollywood." While Dad was a red light, Mom was
a green light, and I was thrilled to go for it. As a fellow
musician and performer, she couldn't help but catch the
excitement. She encouraged me to pursue my dream, and
we formed an unspoken pact. She would help me in any
way she could, and nothing would be said to my father.
We both knew he would not approve.

My mom's musical past was remarkable; I was glad
to have her camaraderie. As a student in the 1930s, she
had been involved with the music program at Abraham
Lincoln High School in Los Angeles while a drama teacher
worked there who was famous for writing musicals and
plays. Many young movie stars attended Abraham because
of him. My mom remembered chatting with people like
Robert Young and Robert Preston in the hallways. The
music director was so impressed with her vocal talent that
he wrote musicals for her to star in. After graduating, she
was approached by two talent scouts—one from Univer-
sal Studios and the other from RKO Pictures.[9] A compe-
tition began, and they both offered her long-term movie
contracts, but she turned them down. "I want to give my
talent to the Lord and sing for Him," she told the scouts.
My mom had been attending church at Angelus Temple[10]
and was Aimee Semple McPherson's soloist in many of
her sacred musicals. In 1924, Sister McPherson founded

---

9   RKO Pictures was an American film production and distribution company. It was one
of the big five studios of Hollywood's Golden Age.

10   Angelus Temple was a domed church in the Echo Park area of Los Angeles funded
mostly through charitable donations for Aimee Semple McPherson's ministry. Touted as
the first megachurch, membership grew to over ten thousand, and Angelus Temple was
advertised as the largest single Christian congregation in the world. According to church
records, the temple received forty million visitors within the first seven years.

KFSG, the first Christian radio station in Los Angeles. She gave my mother two radio shows on that station, where my mom sang songs and invited musical guests to perform. Mom was around eighteen at that time.

Years later, she still loved music, and she was excited that I had the same passion. Whenever I needed to be taken to auditions, she drove me. She even helped to pay for my first recording, "Moon River." Because she kept the family's books, she was able to keep this secret from my father.

Although my demo of "Moon River" was never promoted or played on the radio, it did build my confidence. I played it for the Stansauk twins, who were so impressed they told their manager, Jesse Hodges, about me. Two weeks later, a meeting was arranged at his office in Hollywood. I was so excited I ran into the kitchen and told my mom, who hugged me and agreed to take me there.

The trip to Hollywood took thirty minutes. It was a weekday when other kids my age were at school and my father was at work. My mom dropped me off at the curb and told me she'd be back in an hour to pick me up. Jesse Hodges's office was in a single-story complex that stretched from the street to Sunset Boulevard. A huge globe with the words "Crossroads of the World" greeted me as I walked down the sidewalk leading into the courtyard. I found Jesse's office in the back corner and was surprised there was no reception area to greet me.

Instead, Jesse sat alone at a desk surrounded by light paneled walls and green shag carpet. He was rifling through paperwork but quickly rose to his feet and shook my hand when he saw me walk in. He was a medium-sized man in his forties with dark glasses and an energetic smile. Rather than going back to his desk, he asked me to take a seat and pulled up a chair next to me. I introduced myself as Tommy Thompson—a stage name I had come up with—and he began talking to me as if I were an adult. I took an immediate liking to him.

When he asked about my background and experience, I explained that I had grown up in church and had been coached by my mother, who had been a professional singer. Then I shared about my time in the high-school choir with the Stansauk twins.

Eager to hear my voice, Hodges asked me to stand and sing whatever I was comfortable with. Even though I was familiar with singing a few rock 'n' roll songs, I chose "You'll Never Walk Alone" from the musical *Carousel*, a song my mom had taught me and I had mastered in choir. This was long before the days of karaoke, so I sang a capella, trying to sound confident as I boomed out the familiar tune.

When I finished, Jesse sat tapping his pen on his chin. "You have talent," he said, "but your voice needs to be trained. We need to undo what you've learned in church and start from the very beginning. You need to learn how to talk-sing."

I didn't say anything, but my confused expression must have given me away.

"It's a way of singing that vocalizes the notes much like you're having a conversation with your audience," he explained. "You're used to holding your audience at a distance. But you need to have a more intimate, personal approach. You need to be trained away from that stiff performance posture."

While this idea was foreign to me, it made perfect sense. I was eager to do anything to become a singing sensation.

It turns out Jesse Hodges was not only a manager but also a voice coach. He said he would take me on as a pupil for fifty dollars a session—adding up to two hundred dollars a month or more.

Where am I going to get that kind of cash? I was determined to find a way. "Okay, Mr. Hodges," I said out loud. "I'd love to try."

"Just call me Jesse," he said, walking me to the door. "I'll see you next week. Same time."

When my mom picked me up, I was so excited I talked the whole way home. She agreed to provide the money for my lessons. "We don't need to say anything to your father about this just yet," she added.

During the weekly sessions, Jesse picked the songs to work on. The background music played on a reel-to-reel in his office, and then he'd take me through each part of the song we were working on until he was satisfied. When I was ready, he'd take me into the studio to record a demo. Working in the studio was thrilling. Jesse planned to make me an overall entertainer—similar to a Las Vegas singer. We worked on all kinds of popular music from rock 'n' roll to ballads and jazz.

By the time I was sixteen, Jesse had purchased a recording studio and charged me fifty dollars for every session. These times of training and recording were always full of focus and purpose. I truly felt he was invested in me. I was in my element.

~

There is more to becoming a star than just the music. There's also the image. Once Jesse was certain I could learn his style of singing, he sent me to a professional hair stylist to have my hair cut in a style similar to Bobby Darin and Frankie Avalon. He encouraged me to lose weight and buy new clothes so that I could get a series of promotional head shots done for my professional portfolio. In a matter of months, I went from looking like a slightly pudgy high-school sophomore with eyeglasses to a slick Hollywood icon (with contact lenses).

Unfortunately, this new Hollywood look also appealed to my darker side, which was enamored by the sights and sounds that surrounded me. After my sessions with Jesse, I would watch the people on Hollywood Boulevard, the glamorous icons parading up and down the wide sidewalks, confident and sure of themselves. Their fancy cars and rich lifestyles made my humble upbringing look simple and backward in comparison. Now with my new haircut, slimmer physique, and stylish clothes, I felt I was part of it all. I could be one of those glamorous people who everyone adored and envied.

Once I had proven myself faithful and trustworthy to my mother, I hatched a scheme—a blatant lie—to deceive her. I convinced her that Jesse wanted to extend my hour-long sessions to two or three hours without charging extra money. She believed me, and this gave me an hour or two after my singing lessons to join the procession along Hollywood Boulevard. It was such a relief to be out of the house and in this vibrant atmosphere where no one knew me. As I walked down the sidewalk in my wraparound sunglasses, I imagined I was famous and that people were watching me, wanting to be like me. The extra time also gave me opportunities to check out the good-looking guys who seemed to be everywhere. This soon became an obsession—at times more important than my music.

It was the mid-'60s, and Hollywood was far different from the innocent movies it was producing. It was a city steeped in sexual perversion, with gay nightclubs and bars scattered along its side streets. The streets were clean, and there were sidewalk cafés where I would sit and cruise the good-looking guys who walked the boulevard. At first, I played it safe and just watched. But soon, that raging desire took over, and I started following certain guys I was drawn to. Many weren't interested, but others were, and I would begin conversing with them. My whole focus was to manipulate them to do what I wanted. I could suss out the situation by talking to them and sense by their reactions during the conversation whether or not they were a good possibility for sex. Although I was too young to go into the gay bars, I found underage gay nightclubs and hangouts that did not serve alcohol. Some of them provided private rooms for sex.

Neither Jesse nor my mother had any idea what I was up to.

*Mom in her senior year at Abraham
Lincoln High School.*

*Mom (L) in her twenties preparing for her radio show
on KFSG in Los Angeles.*

*Jesse Hodges engineering a recording of
mine in his studio, Hollywood, California, 1965.*

*Recording my first record, "Where Can I Go?"
and "What Good Would It Do?"*

Head shots used to audition for movies, commercials, etc.

12

FEELING NORMAL

During the time I was developing into an entertainer, my parents finally found a school I could attend: the Pasadena Academy in Altadena. This was a small private school run by the Nazarene Church. I can't remember if the school administration knew about my criminal record when they allowed me to attend, but I do remember my mother was very concerned that I find a way to catch up with my peers and graduate on time. With this in mind, she arranged for me to take on an extra load of classes.

It was 1963, and I was in my junior year. I immediately took to Pasadena Academy. It was a relief to be in school again after being confined to my house for over a year. The school had only 125 students, so I found it easy to make friends. No one knew about my past, which gave me the freedom to reinvent myself. I became active in several sports, including baseball, football, basketball, and tennis—all of which helped me to slim down into the image I was striving to achieve for my singing career.

To all who met me, I gave the impression of a confi-

dent and friendly youth who had it all together. But this
was far from true. I was a mess inside, struggling with my
identity and living two different lives. I was still searching
for ways to satisfy my inner cravings for same-sex encounters. However, I limited these pursuits to Hollywood and
put on a mask of normalcy at school. Not to say I didn't
have my fantasies. There was one boy—a popular athlete
in my class—who I secretly lusted after. I plunged my
energies into sports instead of music—not because I was
such a great athlete but to be close to this boy. Fortunately,
I never actively pursued him, and he had no idea of my
inner fantasies. To him, I was just a friend and one of the
guys.

It was like I had both Dr. Jekyll and Mr. Hyde going
on inside me. At school, I was Jekyll, an upstanding and
friendly young man who was liked by his peers and did
well in class. Mr. Hyde didn't come out until I went to
Hollywood for my singing lessons and lingered around
afterward to cruise the boulevard. Jekyll longed for the
innocence of normalcy and purity. For a time, he even
seemed to be gaining strength over Mr. Hyde. It all started
with a freshman golden-haired beauty with freckles. Her
name was Kathy, and the minute my eyes caught sight of
her, I wanted to meet her.

There was just one problem. For the first time in my
life, I couldn't put on my mask of self-confidence. I was
nervous—almost shaking at the thought of approaching her. Where was that outgoing young man who had
no problem approaching strangers? That was Mr. Hyde,

and I wanted nothing to do with him at this moment. Dr. Jekyll, in all his awkwardness, would have to do.

For several days, I tried to figure out a smooth way to meet her, but no ideas came. I finally gained the courage at lunchtime when I saw her standing in the food line with her friends. Taking my place in line behind her, I waited until there was a break in their conversation. Finally, it came. I reached out and tapped her gently on the shoulder. When she turned around and smiled at me, my words spilled out in a tangled mess.

"Hi, there," I said, my voice sounding louder than normal. My hands were shaking, so I stuffed them into my pants pockets. "I haven't seen you around before. Are you new?"

She giggled but not in a way that made me feel small. It was more like a nervous gesture of friendliness. "I'm a freshman, so, yeah, I just started," she said.

Her friends were whispering to each other, but I tried to ignore them. "Oh, you don't look like a freshman." *Ugh*, I thought. *That didn't sound right.* "I'm new too," I stammered, "Uh, but I'm not a freshman. I mean, I'm a junior and transferred in."

She blushed and told me her brother was a junior.

"Really? What's his name? I probably know him."

When she told me his name, the color must have drained from my face. It was the young man I had secretly fantasized over—the one I had joined all the sports teams for. At that moment, my desire for him shrank to almost nothing, and my desire to get to know Kathy became my all-consuming focus. But unlike my former pursuit, my longing to get to know Kathy was real. It wasn't to satisfy a sexual perversion or fantasy. It was something innocent and pure. It made me feel less dirty and disgusting just to be around her. This was new to me, and I was shocked by the reality of what I was feeling.

I still enjoyed a close friendship with her brother, who had an easy way about him and a boyish masculinity that I craved. His friendship helped me to become close to Kathy, and she and I soon became inseparable. It seemed like a miracle when I found out she felt the same way about me. We did everything together and were in each other's company as much as possible. We dated for over a year, the extent of our affection being to hold hands and embrace. It was all very innocent and cleansing for me. I never pursued Kathy for sex because that would have tainted the whole relationship. She had high ethics and morals. I was so focused on her that my same-sex desires had dropped off considerably. Even so, her influence wasn't enough to completely transform my life; I still had never dealt with the issues from my past. Instead, our relationship gave me a sense of normalcy with my classmates.

With Kathy, I felt I was in a completely different world where things were right-side up. When I was a senior in high school, I asked her to marry me. I even gave her an engagement ring. She gladly accepted, and her parents approved as well.

However, during the last half of my senior year, my father announced we were moving to Torrance, over an hour's commute in busy freeway traffic from where Kathy lived. We didn't move until after my graduation, but I was working full time, and I didn't have a car. When I was able to borrow the family car, the distance between us allowed for only occasional visits. At first, I called her almost every day, but she was rarely home. Her mother said she was busy with school or after-school activities. When I asked her mother when I should call back, she wouldn't give me a clear answer. After about a year of this, Kathy's mother told me the truth.

I could tell by her voice that something was wrong. "Wynn, Kathy is seeing someone else, and they've become deeply involved."

Although I expected something had changed, I was shocked and wanted to hear it from Kathy. "Can I at least talk to her?" I asked.

"I don't think that's a good idea," she said.

I was dumbfounded. "I don't know what to say."

"I suggest you not call again," she advised. "Goodbye, Wynn."

I was heartbroken. Getting over Kathy took time, and I drifted back into same-sex pursuits as a way to ease the pain. This was the fifth major loss in my life—not only because I had lost Kathy but also because I had lost my sense of normalcy. Mr. Hyde was back.

～

I was still traveling to Hollywood every week and working with Jesse. We became close in a teacher-student capacity. I felt safe with him and trusted him because I knew he believed I had the talent to make something of myself. Recording demos in his professional studio seemed to open a whole new world for me; suddenly all the work and time I had put in over the past year was amounting to something significant. I was getting closer to becoming a professional singer. I loved everything about the recording process and was learning so much about what I could do with my voice. Jesse even had me record a song that was written by Glen Campbell but had never been released to the public. Glen had given the song to Jesse to use for training purposes in exchange for recording time in his studio.

Cutting demos in Jesse's studio wasn't cheap, so I started working odd jobs to help pay for things. When Jesse's studio became his primary source of income, he decided to devote his full attention to it. This meant that his managing and voice coaching days were over. When he broke the news to me, I was devastated. What was I going to do now? I didn't have a contract with a major recording studio or a record released to the public yet, and now it looked like that might never happen. But that's when Jesse's recording engineer, Don, stepped in.

Don was a young man who was married to a gorgeous model and had career aspirations of being a manager and music producer. Because I already had a good working relationship with him in the studio, I gladly accepted his offer, and he became my new manager. With me as one of his budding artists, Don started Momentum Records, and I was finally able to release my first record—a 45. A song titled "Where Could I Go?"[11] was on the A-side, and

11   You can listen to all the songs I recorded at my YouTube channel, Wynn Cameron: https://www.youtube.com/channel/UCd1ZRtHN3GE5TtunhFfBvdA.

"What Good Would It Do?" was on the B-side. The recording went well, with Don bringing in studio musicians instead of playing prerecorded music. Since I had to pay for the musicians and the studio time, I was only able to record three records.

The day I recorded these two songs, my father was home because it was a Saturday. My mom and I told him we were going to run some errands and shuffled off to the car as if it were a normal day of shopping. Mom waited for me in the studio as I cut the song and was so impressed with how good I sounded that she and I talked of music the whole way home. It was nearly impossible to hide our enthusiasm and joy when we burst through the door. My father was sitting at the kitchen table, reading the newspaper.

"What's all the excitement?" he asked.

An uncomfortable silence fell over us, and my mother paused, considering her options. Should she continue covering things up? It was one thing to remain silent. It was quite another to blatantly lie to her husband's face. She decided to tell him the truth.

"Wynn has been taking singing lessons," she said, trying to keep her voice level, "and today he cut a record."

My father was quiet as I stood by the door, my hand still on the knob. The high I felt after successfully recording my first real 45 had now turned to trepidation and fear.

"How long has this been going on?" my dad asked in a steady voice.

Both Mom and I seemed unsure how to answer.

"Over a year," she admitted.

My dad folded up his newspaper and stared at her, his eyes betraying both hurt and anger. "And when were you planning to tell me?" he asked.

Truth be told, the time never seemed right. As long as we could get away with not telling him, that was what we did. It was our unspoken rule.

But my mom didn't say that. Instead, she tried to convince him that it was a good thing for me to be doing something I was passionate about. I was so talented and focused, she said.

My father let out a long breath that seemed to linger over the room. "Where have these singing lessons been taking place?" he asked.

That's when the whole truth about Jesse Hodges and Don came out. Needless to say, when my father found out about our many clandestine trips to Hollywood, he exploded. Most of his anger was directed at me, his eyes drilling into mine. Not only had I done this behind his back, but I had duped my mother into being my coconspirator.

"Get out of my sight," he said, pointing to the doorway.

I ran into my room, slamming the door behind me. Throwing myself on the bed, I wept bitterly. I had hoped my dad would have been proud of me. But no, there was only his disgust. It felt like a knife thrust deep into my chest. The emotional pain was almost unbearable. Could he stop me from doing what I loved? Could he take that away from me after all the work and expense? A deep gloom fell over me that day, and the rift between my father and me grew into a chasm. I didn't come out of my room for the rest of the day—not even for dinner. And I didn't speak to my father for weeks.

One of my high school prom pictures.

Getting coached as a member of the Pasadena Academy football team in Altadena, California, 1963. I'm number 82.

PART TWO

Rebellion

13

GUATEMALA

Our home remained tense for several days, but once my dad's anger started to thaw, my mom went to work on him. She began explaining why she felt it was good to support me and help me pursue my dream. I could hear them speaking in quiet tones as she worked on his resolve. In the end, the love my father had for my mom became the deciding factor. He simply could not allow the strain to continue in their relationship. He loved my mom deeply and decided it would please God more to make peace with his wife by allowing his son to pursue his dream of becoming a singer.

When my mom told me this, I was so relieved, and I gave her all the credit. This resulted in a closer relationship with my mom, but my relationship with my dad remained strained.

⁓

As my time in Hollywood continued, so did my prowling for homosexual sex around the boulevard. It was during one of these times when I hooked up with a young talent scout from Guatemala named Marco, who worked for a Guatemalan television producer named Danilo Sanchinelli. When I first met Marco, I was only interested in a quick sexual encounter, but then I found that he was a talent scout. So, I gave him my promotional material and my record. I didn't hold out much hope that this would lead to anything, however, because he gave me the impression that he was looking for someone already on their way to stardom.

Several months later, I got a call from Marco offering me an unbelievable opportunity. Danilo Sanchinelli, he said, heard my record and wanted me to come to Guatemala for two weeks so I could perform on his television show and in several theaters, all-expenses-paid! I was thrilled. I had always wanted to travel, but except for Canada, I had never even been out of the States. I was now nineteen and ready to do something big. So after talking this opportunity over with my manager and going over the contract, I eagerly accepted the offer and boarded the plane to Guatemala. I was finally getting the break I needed and was on my way to stardom!

As I sat on the plane heading to Guatemala, I thought about all the hard work I had put in to get to where I was now going—the voice lessons, the sneaking around, the expense, and the time. It was now going to finally pay off. I wondered if I had what it would take to become famous, but I quickly dismissed my doubts. This was my destiny. I was meant for the stage. I could do this. It was all about playing a part and making it seem real—something my double life had already taught me how to do.

In all my years of leading a secret life of same-sex pursuits, I had learned to lie and deceive well. A good actor can make people believe the character they are portraying. I had learned to do that in school, at church, with my friends, and in Hollywood. I knew how to show people what I wanted to show them, and I used that talent to manipulate others to do what I wanted.

⸎

When the Pan Am jet touched down at the Guatemalan City airport and taxied toward the terminal, the other passengers started murmuring in excited whispers. I looked out the small round window of the plane and saw a crowd lined up waving flags and holding signs in Spanish. A large banner with huge, bold letters read "BENVENUTO, WYNN CAMERON." Stunned, I stared in amazement at the cheering crowd. Wynn Cameron was my stage name, but how did these people know who I was? Who were they? And why were they cheering for me? It was like the best dream I had ever had—only it was real!

"Who's that? It must be someone famous," I overheard one of the passengers ask.

Then a voice came over the plane's loudspeakers: "Wynn Cameron, please exit at the rear of the plane."

A young stewardess walked up to my seat and asked me to follow her. The people near me watched as she led me to the back of the plane where a set of stairs were lowered near the waiting fanfare. As I walked across the tarmac to the cheering crowd, I was thoroughly enjoying the attention. A camera and news crew from the local TV station filmed me greeting the people in the crowd, and then Marco stepped up, laughing while he shook my hand.

"Surprised?" he asked over the crowd's cheering.

I was speechless. All I could do was smile and nod my head.

"This is nothing. Just wait," he said.

Marco ushered me away from the crowd and into the terminal, where my passport was stamped.

It was a surreal experience and completely unexpected. I soon discovered that Danilo had arranged for my two singles to be played over the radio throughout Guatemala and other neighboring countries. He had already built up a fan base for me, setting the stage for my visit.

We left the airport in a string of cars—me sitting with Marco in a white stretch limousine. The interior of the limo was brown leather with plush carpeting and a table between us.

The limo took us to Hotel Imperador in Guatemala City. I felt like royalty as I followed Marco through the fancy hotel lobby. A uniformed bellboy carried my luggage and led us to a large suite on the second floor.

Marco helped me unpack and then ushered me out to the waiting limo to take me to a practice session with the local rock 'n' roll band Los Rocks. They would be backing me up during my tour, he explained. After introductions at the studio, we only had a short time to practice because I had my first show in a theater downtown that very night.

~

There was a large audience waiting at the theater

when we arrived. I was nervous because I didn't know the songs very well and had to read the music and words as I sang. Needless to say, I was embarrassed. But the audience seemed to love the show anyway—even with my less-than-stellar performance.

Later that night at the hotel, Marco handed me a tape recorder, telling me to practice some new songs I would be performing in two days.

"Just learn the words and the music," he explained. "We'll go over the details of the performance and let you practice the dance moves later at the studio."

Danilo came to the hotel with Marco the following day to introduce himself. He was a stocky middle-aged man with bushy black hair. Although he smiled a lot and tried to speak English, I had trouble understanding him and felt uneasy around him. In broken English, he explained that I would not only be performing on his television show, *Ritmos de la Juventud* (Rhythm of the Youth), but he had also booked performances throughout Guatemala and other Central American countries where my songs were gaining in popularity. I could hardly take it in. Before Guatemala, I had never performed in front of a live audience except in church and as a member of my high-school choir. I was nervous but also very excited.

For the next forty-eight hours, I did almost nothing but learn the songs they had given me. The show was live, so I had only one shot at this. I reviewed everything: the suit I would be wearing, my hair, my expression, and how I would move onstage while singing. I didn't want to appear like a shy kid from California who didn't know what he was doing. I needed to exude confidence and appeal—as though I were already famous and had done this a hundred times before. There was a large mirror over the bureau in my hotel room, and I practiced in front of it over and over, making sure my moves and facial expressions were right as I belted out the songs that were playing on the recorder.

Two days later, Marco picked me up from the hotel and drove me to the television studio. It was a large, cavernous building with a set that could be used for multiple purposes, including a local news program and other shows. Danilo gave me instructions, his wide grin exposing a gold canine tooth. In addition to me, there was a group of four young American girls called Las Go-Go Girls, who performed on his show as dancers and backup singers— all hoping to make it big someday. They would be dancing with me while I sang. As I was introduced to the teenage girls, I said under my breath, "It's good to meet you. I'm so glad to have others here who I can speak English with." They smiled and agreed. The only Spanish I knew were the words I had learned in my high school Spanish class.

I walked around the stage and oriented myself. I was operating on pure adrenalin and hoped my face didn't betray what a novice I was. I did my best to look like a seasoned performer—calm, cool, and collected. *This is just routine,* I told myself. *You've done this hundreds of times.* Well, I hadn't. But I could pretend.

I waited in a small dressing room as audience members began taking their seats. Danilo didn't want me to linger around the set during this time because they were going to present me as a star, not as some wide-eyed novice. His show was a combination of interviews and performances, and I was to be the third act. I was relieved that I wouldn't be interviewed. Still, I knew I had to make this performance count, and the waiting was excruciating.

Then a burst of music and a booming voice announced the show as the audience erupted in cheers and clapping. I could feel my heart pounding through the first act. Then Marco came into the dressing room halfway into the second act.

"Are you ready?"

"Absolutely," I said.

I followed him to the stage entrance, all the while trying to still my shaking hands.

I couldn't understand anything the man onstage was saying, but as soon as he called out my name, the audience burst into a roar of clapping and cheering. The opening music to the song blared as I walked onstage and grabbed the microphone. I could barely see anything because the stage lights were so bright. Las Go-Go Girls surrounded me, and as soon as I started singing, the audience quieted down and began clapping to the beat of the song. Although I still felt a little stiff, their clapping and chanting helped me to relax and enjoy myself. By the time the song finished, I was high on adrenalin and grinning in exultation. They loved me! What a rush!

Looking back, I think that performance was probably a little raw and stiff, but the audience didn't seem to notice, and neither did Danilo. He booked me on two more shows and then started setting up performances across different cities in Guatemala. All the while, my two songs were being played over the radio and gaining popularity.

Danilo also set up several radio interviews. A DJ at one of these interviews asked me to perform from the station's balcony suite studio. At first, I felt a little conspicuous, standing on the balcony with microphone in hand. But as soon as the music blared out and I began singing, a large crowd formed in the street below. Even the traffic stopped as people came out of their cars to listen. No one seemed upset by the impromptu concert. Instead, a party atmosphere ensued, with people waving their hands in the air and clapping.

After the performance, there were so many people lingering about that I had to wait nearly two hours before I could safely leave the building. Finally, Marco had me follow him down the sidewalk. Seconds later, the sound of running footsteps came from behind us. A large group of girls was heading our way! We started running to get away from them, but they caught up with us and began pulling and tearing at my clothes to get anything they could for a souvenir. Marco shoved me through a shop entrance, closing and locking the door behind us. We stayed there until he could figure out a way to get me safely back to my hotel suite.

~

By the time we started touring and doing shows, I was more confident in my performances. Remembering an old movie about Al Jolson, a Vaudeville performer in the 1920s and '30s who loved to personally connect with his audience, I decided to do the same. My stage crew thought I was crazy when I asked for a four-hundred-foot microphone cord. No one had ever requested anything like that before, the stage manager told me. I didn't tell him why I wanted it because I wanted to surprise him and all who would be attending the show. As I performed the first song, I sang with the mic on its stand. Then, as the second verse of the second song came up, I suddenly pulled the mic away from the stand and jumped off the stage in front of the audience. The audience screamed in delight as I walked up the left aisle while singing to individuals in the crowd. This was a personal touch that was almost unheard of in 1966 concert performances, but I was a natural. For me, this was what performing was all about. I loved looking people in the eyes as I sang to them. Getting off the stage and going out to them was the only way I could do this. Everyone—especially the band members who were touring with me—was shocked by the excitement and momentum it drew. It quickly became one of my signature moves and was wildly popular with the fans and the local media.

～

Along with my sudden rise to stardom came the parties and the drinking. Temptations were everywhere, and I quickly found myself reverting to my old habits of seducing young men. I was very subtle, and my cravings were unquenchable. I loved everything about the Spanish culture of Latin America and indulged in the food, drinks, and party life. Yet when it was time for practice or my performances, I was always ready, sober, and eager to jump onstage. I was living the life of a star and reveling in the hedonistic joys of self-fulfillment.

And just when I thought I had arrived, it occurred to me that I hadn't been paid. True, my living expenses were covered, but I had yet to see any actual money from my performances or royalties from my songs that were being aired. After my two-week contract was up, I approached Danilo for payment. He made excuses and brushed me off. I didn't give up, however, and asked him several more times about our agreement for compensation. He never gave me any money, though. Then I found out most of his young performers—including Las Go-Go Girls and the band Los Rocks—were never paid their due compensation.

Suddenly, I no longer felt like a star but a fool. Had I really been duped into coming all this way only to make Danilo a pile of money? I appealed to Marco, but he wouldn't talk about it. "You need to talk to Danilo," he said.

Marco became scarce, and I hardly ever saw him after that. What was I going to do? I wasn't ready to go home because I was famous in Guatemala. In the three months I had been there my songs had hit the top of the music charts. I had learned conversational Spanish and had made many friends. One of these was a young man named Julio who came from a family that owned a large coffee plantation near the border of Mexico. His family was excited about my music and my sudden fame. They offered to take me in after my fallout with Danilo. I started living in their beautiful home in the city and visiting their plantation, where I met and befriended many Guatemalan natives who were of Mayan Indian descent.

Julio's older brother, Marcus, and his friend Rubio took me to El Salvador to get a one-year visa for Guatemala. They were also able to open doors to many venues in other Central American countries. Eventually, one of the largest cigarette and beer companies in the country took notice and offered to provide promotions and finance my touring. They even started negotiations for me to do my own hour-long TV show with a one-year contract. However, Danilo was a lot more powerful than I ever gave him credit for. When he found out about this, he somehow discouraged the company owners from following through with their offer. I was able to stay in Guatemala for three months until I ran too low on money. It soon became unavoidable—I would have to return to the States. I still had my plane ticket home, but I had to pay extra for my baggage, which took every cent I had plus more that I had to borrow.

It broke my heart to leave. And it was so ironic that just when my songs were the number-one and number-two hits in Central America, I was returning to the United States penniless and broken. I never did see one cent of royalties from those songs even though they remained at the top of the charts for six months. My manager could do nothing to help because there was no international agreement and protection on contracts in the 1960s.[12]

---

12 It wasn't unusual for artists to be taken advantage of in other countries in the 1960s. Many of the biggest stars—including the Beatles and the Rolling Stones—lost hundreds of thousands of dollars until international laws were signed and passed by most countries to protect artists and abide by contractual agreements.

My performance on the TV show Ritmos de la Juventud
(Rhythm of the Youth), Guatemala, 1966.

Singing from the balcony of a radio station in Guatemala.

Las Go-Go Girls, Los Rocks, and me on the road in Guatemala.

*Danilo Sanchinelli (front row, center), Los Rocks,
and me (middle row, center) before our next show.*

*Signing autographs with one of my band members
after a live show in El Salvador.*

*In Guatemala, just before jumping
offstage to sing and walk through the audience.*

A photo handout given to those attending my concerts in Central America, 1966.

The backside of the handout.

14

COMING HOME

When I arrived home from Guatemala, I sank into depression. My adventures with fame and misfortune felt more like a dream, and here I was back in reality—unemployed and living with my parents. Through it all, my mom and dad seemed relieved that I was home safe. I suspect they were silently hoping I would find my bearings, learn life's lessons, and mature into a man of good character. But I had other plans.

Even with the devastating effects of being used and cheated in Guatemala, I had tasted stardom, and I wasn't ready to give up on that dream. I continued working with Don Perry and Momentum Records in finding a song to record—one that would get airtime on radio stations. But I had no money to make this happen. Although I was living at home and not paying rent, my mom no longer offered to help me financially, and I knew better than to ask. Instead, I got a job. My father managed a warehouse that supplied records for department stores, and he used his contacts to help me find work at May Company. With the money I made working in the men's clothing section of the store, I was able to save enough to finance another recording and buy a used car. Now I could travel between Torrance and Hollywood without relying on family members for a ride.

Unfortunately, I also had another way of making money. I was experimenting with marijuana and selling it on the side.

Eventually, Don found a song for me to record titled "Up, Down," which had been rejected by the Lovin' Spoonful.[13] Don had it arranged in my key, with the basic tracks laid out so that I could go into the studio and sing. My brother, Brian, who was fascinated by the show business industry, came with me the day I was recording. As I showed him around the studio, he pulled out his camera and started taking pictures. He seemed preoccupied, so I found a moment to get alone.

"Hey, I'll be right back," I told him. "I left the words to the song in the car."

This wasn't true. I was going back to the car so that I could smoke a joint and relax. Everything was riding on this new record, and I thought marijuana would help me sing better. Neither Brian nor Don had any idea what I was up to.

After recording "Up, Down," things began to spiral.

13   An American rock band popular during the 1960s. It is best known for the hits "Summer in the City" and "Do You Believe in Magic."

The recording sounded good, and we were pleased with how it came out, but there was no money for promotion. So the record was never aired by the radio stations.

Eventually, I got tired of living at home and found a roommate and a place to live in Hollywood. I wanted to be closer to my manager and live in an environment where everything was happening. I started pursuing acting along with singing.

But things were stagnant in my quest for fame, and feelings of being used and abused flared up. I felt worthless. I needed to build myself up and turned to the only things that made me feel better; drugs, parties, and orgies soon dominated everything—even my desire to become famous. Instead of realizing that my lifestyle choices were destroying my chances for success, I blamed Don and Momentum Records because they didn't promote my music and lacked the money to fund any new recordings. It was everyone else's fault and no surprise when Momentum went out of business.

My hedonistic lifestyle also conflicted with my job at May Company. I started coming in late and hungover. I was sometimes rude and inattentive to customers. At first, my coworkers covered for me, but my boss soon noticed my underperformance and fired me. I was so caught up in my dysfunction that I didn't even care—except that I needed the income to continue living in Hollywood. I certainly didn't want to move back in with my parents. I was caught in a classic *Catch-22*. I wanted to live in Hollywood so that I could keep partying with my friends, but the party lifestyle prevented me from earning the money I needed to maintain it. What to do?

At first, I tried to rely on my roommate, Tim, to cover my half of the rent until I found another job to pay him back. But then Tim also lost his job. Rent was due, and we had no money.

Like me, Tim was in his early twenties and dipping into the drug and gay lifestyle. We were sitting around our small apartment, trying to determine how we were going to pay rent. We had a small amount of marijuana we could sell but not enough to cover even half of it. Only one option seemed clear, so we smoked a joint and left the apartment, each taking a different side street off Hollywood Boulevard to pick up a customer. It was a warm summer evening as I stood on a dark street corner dressed in tight jeans and a Polo shirt, waiting for a paying customer. Although I had pursued many hookups for fun and excitement, this was different. My gut was cramping, and I was sweating. But I was trying to appear confident. *What am I doing?* I was still high, but not even the marijuana could dull my fear that the next car coming around the corner might be the police—or, worse, a demented pervert.

Just then, a white Cadillac convertible pulled up to the curb, and a good-looking man in his forties asked me if I needed a lift.

"Only if you do . . . for fifty?" I said, indicating my intentions.

"Hop in," he said in a friendly manner and smiled as I jumped over the door and into his car.

Although I was trying to mask my nervousness, he must have noticed because he started asking questions. "How old are you?" he said. "Why are you on the street?"

When I told him, he shook his head and said, "You're too young to be doing this. Here." He pulled a fifty-dollar bill from his wallet and put it in my hand. Then he drove me home. "Get off the street," he said as I climbed out of his car. "You don't need to be doing this."

Incredibly, Tim came home thirty minutes later with another fifty-dollar bill and almost the same story! To this day, I believe God was watching over us, trying to warn us away from where we were heading. Unfortunately, neither of us was listening. Instead, when we fell short on cash again, we did the same thing. This time we were not so lucky and had to earn our keep.

After a few months of this, I had had enough and moved back in with my parents.

Unfortunately, this didn't stop my behavior. I began searching for gay bars along the beaches, but no matter what I found or who I was with, I couldn't satisfy my need for masculine identity, affirmation, and touch.

I began hanging out with a group of friends—both gay and straight—who were saturated in the drug lifestyle. We had LSD parties and contests to see who could have the wildest hallucinations. Over the next few years, I took over three hundred hits of LSD. At one point, my friends and I were in Long Beach dropping LSD when we decided to drive to a nightclub on the Sunset Strip in West Holly-wood. As we walked out of the house and down the path, the ivy on each side of the cement path appeared to be moving. I looked closer and saw each leaf opening and closing like green mouths. Despite my hallucinations, I insisted on driving because we were taking my car, but I was having difficulty focusing. The freeway stretched out before me like a long tunnel. The ceiling of the tunnel was a glowing kaleidoscope of colors, swirling all around. It's a miracle I didn't cause an accident. When we got to the nightclub, I was so high I didn't want to go in. I was content to sit in the car and watch the tall buildings near the nightclub melt down and then rebuild themselves over and over again.

My parents had no idea about the risks I was taking during this time. But years later, my mom told me about how God had impressed her to pray fervently for my safety.

In the studio recording "Up, Down," 1967.

Refining "Up, Down" with my manager, Don Perry.

15

BACK TO SCHOOL

Because I was living at home and didn't have to pay for room or board, I managed to support my addictions by working a few sales jobs near Hollywood. Knowing that I would be better off away from there, my parents urged me to find work locally. Then a job in the most unexpected place materialized. Little did I realize that this job, which I was surprisingly qualified for, would prove to be a shadow of my true calling.

I was still pursuing my sex, drug, and rock 'n' roll lifestyle, coming home at all hours of the night, stumbling about, reeking of alcohol and marijuana. My parents were bewildered, but they said nothing and struggled through it. When my mom found out about a little Christian school in need of a sixth-grade teacher, she recommended me for the position. She was friends with the school's principal and must have been convincing, because they asked me to apply.

I was ready for a change as well. Bored with the menial jobs I continued to hold for a time and then lose, I thought this might be the distraction I needed to focus my attention on something more positive. The pay was low, but I wanted to prove to my parents that I could do something good. Their opinions of me—especially my mom's opinion—really mattered. She had gone out of her way to recommend me, and I thought maybe this would help me to make up for at least some of the wrong I had done to her in the past. I owed her that much.

In the time before the new semester began, I struggled through reading the textbooks, but the material seemed easy enough. I told myself I would give it my all—the best I could do—and if the kids didn't show signs of learning after their first six-week report cards came out, I would quit.

But as I made my way to the classroom, I was having second thoughts. A slow learner myself, how was I going to teach these kids? Then it occurred to me: I was very good at playing a part and entertaining an audience. This would be just like that. I would play the part of a teacher— the kind of teacher I would have responded to when I was a kid. By the time I reached the door, I knew what I had to do: exude the same confidence I had demonstrated while performing in Guatemala.

The kids were running and jumping around the classroom when I walked in, throwing wads of paper across the room and cheering when they hit their opponents. Desks were clumped together in the middle of the classroom. I walked in with the principal, an older woman with cat-eye horned glasses and a congenial but stern disposition. The kids didn't seem to notice our entrance until the principal started writing my name on the chalkboard. Then they calmed down and started taking their seats. Wadded-up paper was strewn across the floor, and the students made no effort to move their desks or pick up the trash.

"Class," the principal said, "this is your new teacher, Mr. Thompson. You need to give him the respect he deserves so that you can learn from him. I expect you to act like the ladies and gentlemen our good Lord has created you to be."

The students looked bored but also a little curious. They were probably puzzled by my appearance. In my stylish 1970s clothes and longer hair, I didn't look like the typical teacher. I was very young—in my early twenties—and this seemed to intrigue them.

"Now pick up the trash and set your desks in order," the principal continued. "This is not anarchy, after all. This is a place of learning."

Most of the students complied, but a few stayed at their desks, talking and laughing with each other in whispers.

Fear of what I was about to take on began rising within me. I pushed it down and strode in front of the chalkboard. Nodding to the principal, I said, "Thank you, Mrs. Plies. I can take it from here."

She looked relieved and left the room.

I wanted to be on friendly terms with these kids, but I also needed to have their respect. And how was I going to accomplish that? To be honest, I didn't have a plan—only that I had six topics to teach every day.

As I awkwardly stood in front of the class, I addressed

them. "My name is Mr. Thompson, and as you can see, I'm not a normal teacher."

A few of the girls giggled, and I cleared my throat. "I mean this won't be like any class you've ever been in."

The students looked puzzled but interested.

"I like to be creative, and I think you like that as well, so this isn't going to be the same old boring class you've experienced in the past." I paused, looking at each of their faces. "Are you game for something different?"

The entire class seemed to come alive as heads nodded and hands were raised into the air. I called on a tall redheaded boy sitting in the back.

"What do you mean by 'different'?" he asked.

I smiled mysteriously. "You'll just have to find out as we go through the semester."

Getting my students to pay attention was the biggest challenge I faced, and I tried coming up with creative solutions. One day, I brought my guitar to school. I was playing in a band at the time and thought the guitar might pique their interest. As soon as I took it out of the case, I had their attention.

I began strumming a simple tune and then sang out, *"Does anyone know what a fraction is?"*

The students laughed, but no one said anything.

"Does anyone know what a fraction is?" I sang out again.

This time, a tall, lanky boy in the back of the room sang out loudly, *"A fraction is a number less than one."*

The class erupted in laughter.

"That's right!" I sang, motioning the kids to repeat me.

"That's right!" several of them sang back.

The students were laughing, but I had their attention.

"And what is another way a number can be less than one?" I sang.

A girl with braces in the front row eagerly raised her hand. I nodded to her.

"Could it be a decimal?" she sang out in perfect tune.

"That's right!" I sang, again motioning for the class to repeat me.

"That's right!" they sang back.

I sang through the entire math lesson, encouraging them to participate. Unconventional, yes. But it was working. My students got such a kick out of these kinds of antics that they started learning and doing their work. From then on, I sang one lesson to them every week.

On warm days, we ventured outside and sat in the ball field in front of the school. My students loved getting out of the stuffy classroom and were on their best behavior as I taught while sitting with them in a circle. Was it my young age, my unconventional methods, God's grace, or all of the above that helped me to succeed? I'm not sure. But somehow I was able to connect with those kids.

One of my most successful ways of challenging them came when I changed the grading curve. Instead of the traditional curve, I decided my students had to get at least 95 percent to earn an A and 85 percent to earn a B. I didn't tell them I had changed the curve; I just did it. When they came to me with complaints and questions about why their grades had dropped, I encouraged them by saying, "You can do this!" For some reason, they took on the challenge with no further complaints. My greatest success was with one little African American girl who had failing grades. I kept encouraging her to try harder, and after six weeks, she went from an F to a B-plus. After getting her report card, she came to school with her parents. They were elated and shook my hand. "I don't know what you're doing, but keep doing it because she's learning," her father told me.

To be honest, I didn't know either. I think they sensed I cared about them and believed in them, and it had a positive effect on their performance.

Although teaching at that little school was a full-time job, the pay was very low, and I wanted to earn more money. So I also worked as a security guard from 10:30 p.m. until 6:30 a.m. Monday through Friday. Instead of sleeping after school, I used this time to practice with my band in my parents' garage. Needless to say, my schedule was crazy, with little time for sleep. It went like this: I worked all night and then went straight to the school, changing my clothes there. After school, I practiced with my band for two hours. Then I went to bed for three hours. I got up, showered, shaved, dressed, and quickly drove to my night security job and started the twenty-four-hour cycle all over again. I barely slept until the weekend. While working my security job, I would grade papers from my teaching job and catch catnaps between making my rounds. To make up for my lack of sleep, I popped pills—uppers, or, as we called them, bennies.

In addition to my two jobs, I was also selling marijuana

and satisfying my sexual appetite with other guys. Other than taking bennies to stay awake, I kept myself clean while working at the school. I never pursued my sexual appetites there, nor did I sell any marijuana at the school or to my students.

But it was only a matter of time before my two lives collided.

It happened one evening while I was happily smoking a joint in my car at Hermosa Beach before going up to my friend Sam's apartment. Sam and I had an easy friendship of music and marijuana, sometimes partying through the night with a few others. I often stayed overnight on the weekends so that I could party to my heart's content without my parents around to witness the aftermath. As I leaned my head out the open window to expel the smoke from my lungs, a small man in flip-flops and shorts approached. He stooped toward the open window and sniffed.

"Hey, you got any more of that? I have money," he said.

I did have four other joints in my car, but I was streetwise by then and never sold drugs to anyone I didn't know.

"No, sorry. This is all I have," I said.

At that point, he reached into his shorts pocket and pulled out a small leather billfold. Opening it, he showed me his badge.

"Step out of the car, please," he said mechanically.

"What for?" I asked. As far as I could tell, I hadn't done anything wrong.

The officer opened the door, and I stepped out. Then

he searched my car and found the four joints. "I thought you said you didn't have anymore," he said, holding them up for me to see.

"Well, they aren't for sale," I said.

But this didn't matter. The use of marijuana was still illegal. He wrote me up and took me to jail for possession of marijuana.

Since this was my first drug offense, the judge dropped the charges. However, I lost my teaching position because of it. The hardest part was breaking the news to my mom.

I waited until I could tell her in person. After explaining what happened, I could see the disappointment on her face. "I'll admit I thought you were done with that," she said. "You were so busy working two jobs I didn't realize it was still going on."

What could I say? I had no excuses, so I waited for her to continue.

"Now those kids are going to need a teacher," she said, resignation in her voice. "Since I'm the one who got you the position, I'm responsible for what happens to them. I'll offer to take your place and teach them myself."

While I felt guilty about this, I was also relieved. I knew my students would be in good hands with my mom teaching them. She was a natural when it came to teaching.

"I'm sorry, Mom," I finally said. "I know I let you down. But I really liked teaching."

"I know," she said. "I could tell."

Before she took over, I told her about the new grading system I had created and how successful it was.

"They're used to it now, and they're working harder," I explained.

She was visibly impressed and kept the grading curve the same way. Mom fulfilled my obligation until the end of the school year, with most of the class moving on to the next grade level with an A or B average.

⁓

I never thought too much about how my behavior was affecting my parents. The strain must have been almost unbearable for them, and yet they bore it. I was depressed and struggled between the selfish, hedonistic, false mask I hid behind and the real Wynn, who was struggling to find a foothold in life.

In the last seven years of her life, Mom told me a story about how all this was affecting her. It was after I had lost my job at the school, and she was working full time as my replacement. I was having band practice with my friends in the garage, and she had just arrived home after a long day at school. My bandmates and I were so clueless, thinking no one could smell the weed if we kept the garage door shut, but she could smell it and hear us—our laughter, foul language, and beers being popped open.

She pushed her way through the front door with an armful of books and school supplies. Overwhelmed by the burden, she dropped the books and crumpled to the carpet.

"Forgive me, Lord," she prayed. "I just can't love him anymore."

She lost all composure, her eyes and nose running with her cries of anguish. As she eventually regained control of her emotions, the room became still, and she heard a voice in her head as clear as if Jesus were in the room speaking to her.

"That's okay, honey," He said. "Just let Me love him through you."

She told me her whole perspective changed toward me after that day as if a great load was lifted from her. She would need that strength to get through everything in the coming years with grace and love.

My sixth-grade class.
I'm standing in the center-back row.

*Getting ready to practice with my band
at our house in Torrance, California.*

*In Hermosa Beach, California, where I
stayed with my friend Sam.*

16

JAIL 1969

After losing my job as a teacher, I moved to an upstairs bungalow apartment near the beach so I could spend time with friends, playing music and doing drugs. I paid my rent and financed my lifestyle by selling drugs. My drug of choice was speed, which helped me to feel like I was on top of the world and in control of everything. Without my parents' watchful eyes nearby, I was dealing drugs and pursuing my sexual appetites without constraint. I was constantly on the prowl, and it was only a matter of time before I was caught. This time the officers showed up at my door with a warrant for my arrest: felony drug and sex charges.

~

The judge spoke clearly while declaring my sentence. "One year in the LA County Jail, with up to three months for good behavior."

Bewildered, I turned to my lawyer, who asked if I understood the sentence.

"Please tell me again," I said, my voice barely audible.

My lawyer said I should be grateful. Because this was my first big offense on drug and sex charges, the judge had suspended a three-year county jail sentence to only one year with three years' probation.

But I wasn't thankful; I was terrified. I had heard about the LA County Jail, how it was filled with hardened criminals waiting to be transferred into the federal prison system.

I looked around the courtroom, not recognizing a single face. When I had been a juvenile offender, my parents had always been required to accompany me to court. Thank God I was now twenty-three and could spare them this humiliation. I was relieved I didn't have to witness their forlorn expressions and grateful they were not there to see mine.

I waited as an officer cuffed me and ushered me out of the courtroom. We walked down a long hallway to a stairwell that descended to the courthouse basement. The pungent smells of urine and body odor were inescapable. I was placed into a large holding cell crowded with drunks sleeping on cold metal benches, older men looking disheveled and weary, tattooed younger men with hardened faces, and those like me: pale, avoiding eyes, dejected, and frightened.

I thought about my life and all the things I had done that had led up to this moment. *How could I have been so stupid? What was I thinking?* Fear and disgrace engulfed me as I sat on one of the cold benches and put my face in my hands. Cruel words from the past rang through my head.

It was the voice of the woman officer who had booked me into jail when I was only fourteen years old. I was seeing her again as if she were standing right in front of me, disgust and revulsion riddling her face. "I would *never* allow you to play with *my* children." The weight of her statement so many years ago pushed down hard on me. *That's me,* I thought. *She was right. I deserve all this because I'm worse than rubbish.* My heart raced, and my breathing quickened. There was no escaping it—I was doomed. I couldn't stop thinking about all the terrible things that had been done to me and the terrible things I had done to others.

Suddenly, an officer's sharp command jerked me back into the moment. "When your name is called, line up."

I waited as he ran down the list, and then I fell in line with the others when I heard my name. The officers shackled our wrists and ankles and then led us single file into the parking lot, where a bus was waiting to take us to the county jail. As I walked outside shackled with the others, I felt my legs grow weak. Afraid I would collapse in line, I quickly boarded the bus and found a seat. *This is crazy. This isn't who I am,* I thought. Everything I held dear—my dreams of fame, my friends, my talent, my charisma—was stripped away. What remained was too horrible to consider.

A large man with dark skin took the seat next to me, and I turned away and looked out the small barred window. The bus began moving, and the Torrance courthouse drifted out of sight. I was about to spend a year behind bars. How was I going to bear it?

◞

Upon arriving at the Los Angeles County Hall of Justice, the bus went down into the basement parking. The building was constructed in 1925 and had fourteen floors. The first ten floors were administrative offices, and the top four floors were the old LA County Jail. Guards yelled at us as we left the bus and were led like a herd of cattle into a basement room, where we were unshackled and told to strip down. We put our clothes in paper bags and then handed them to a guard, who wrote our last names and our issued jail numbers on the bags with a thick black marker. Once naked, we were led into a large shower area and hosed off. Then we were sprayed with white powder— some kind of disinfectant, I suspect. Naked and covered in powder, we waited in line for the cavity search. Each of us was forced to bend over in front of the others while a guard searched for drugs and other paraphernalia in the most private of places. Any last refuge of human dignity we may have felt up to that point had now vanished.

Next, we were issued blue jeans, underwear, and white T-shirts stamped with "LA County Jail" across the front in bold black letters. I suited up as quickly and quietly as possible, not wishing to bring any attention to myself. The guards yelled a lot, threatening to throw us into the hole—a dark cell without windows—if anyone spoke or made a sound during this initial processing time. There was no doubt they meant every word.

After standing in line and listening to them shout out the rules, we were led to the back stairwell and started climbing the stairs. Once we reached the second floor of the jail, the guards led several prisoners out to their cells. My cell was on the third floor. I followed the guard to my new home: a twenty-four-square-foot area enclosed by bars on all sides, containing two bunk beds and a toilet. There were no walls between cells—only bars—and no privacy. Not even to use the toilet. Each cell housed up to four inmates.

The iron gate of my cell slammed shut behind me and I stood frozen for a few seconds. My two cellmates regarded me with disinterest as I made my way over to an empty bed and started spreading out the sheets and blanket provided by the jail. Then I lay down on the thin mattress and turned on my side. *How will I ever get through this? God, I'm so sorry for all I've done. Please help me,* I prayed silently. But my prayers seemed to be going no farther than the ceiling. Maybe God knew what was really in my heart. Terrified and filled with shame, yes. But repentant? Not so much. *Where is He?* I wondered. *Has He totally abandoned me?* A weight of depression overcame me.

I tried to avoid the faces of my cellmates, but it was impossible to do so in such close quarters. They were lingering about like the walking dead—only hardness and anger. How was I going to handle this in the days and months to come? What would I be like when I was finally released?

I didn't sleep much that first night. It was cold, and the smell of strong body odor assaulted my nostrils. I needed another blanket, but I was afraid to ask for one. There were strange human sounds and weird noises all night long, and I could only wonder about what was happening in the other cells. I asked God to help me even though I knew I didn't deserve it. All I could sense was thick darkness. *If demons are real, they're most certainly in this place,* I thought, shivering.

~

I don't remember sleeping that first night, but I must have finally drifted off, because I was awakened by a guard yelling, "Mealtime. Line up." We were led through a maze of barred cells, down the dark stairwell, to the mess hall—a large room filled with metal tables and benches. After going through the food line, where inmate kitchen workers slopped portions of overcooked food onto our meal trays, we quickly sat and scarfed down our food. There was no time to talk or get acquainted; the only purpose of mealtime was to eat whatever we could manage in seven minutes. After that, we were ordered to get up and dump any remaining food into the trash so that another group of inmates could take our places. The food was tasteless, but I did my best to eat everything so that I wouldn't go hungry.

Other than mealtimes and the occasional shower, there was little break in my routine. I sat in my cell with absolutely nothing to do to pass the time. Minutes dragged on like hours, and the only resource I could take advantage of were the library books provided by the jail. So even though I wasn't much of a reader due to my dyslexia, I eagerly struggled through as many books as I could get my hands on.

One morning before dawn, I was jarred awake by deafening screams echoing down the cell blocks. Lights went on, and confusion reigned as cell bars banged and earsplitting wails echoed off the walls. It finally became quiet again after an hour, and the lights were turned off. *What happened?* I fought to calm my mind and fall back asleep. I didn't find out until the next day when I heard through the jailhouse grapevine that one inmate tried to rape his cellmate, and a fight had ensued, leaving one man badly injured and the other man dead.

For the next several days, the mood throughout the jail was tense. The death of an inmate was not a common occurrence, but rape and sexual activity were. Although I wanted to dabble in these sexual opportunities, I certainly didn't want to be raped. So I kept myself in check. Shower time posed the greatest threat because groups of prisoners showered together, and rapes often occurred. By the second week, I had heard so many stories of rape that I was always on guard. Fortunately, it never happened to me.

After a few months, a guard stood in front of our cell and asked if anyone knew how to type.

I looked up from my bed, where I was reading. "I know how."

"Good," the guard said. "Come with me."

He took me down to the first floor of the jail and put

me in front of a manual typewriter. Then he told me to
type out what he read.

After looking over the lines of type I had just produced,
the guard nodded. "You'll do just fine," he said.

To my surprise, I was moved down to the first floor
and given a typing job in a small office next to the medical
wing. In addition to typing up records, I was expected to
listen for problems with the patients housed in the medical
wing and notify the authorities if anything went wrong.
Not only did this give me something to do during the
day, but this job also allowed me to have a private cell on
the first floor. No longer did I have to live out in the open
where every move I made was seen by other prisoners and
guards. Now I had a private walled room all to myself.
The room had two windows where guards could look in,
but it felt so much better than the communal living I had
been forced to endure on the third floor.

Unfortunately, this newfound freedom also gave me
license to practice my predator instincts. I took notice of
who was coming into the medical wing and set my sights
on a few of the younger, good-looking guys. This was no
easy task because I had to plan how to get close to them
and then plan where we could have sex and how I could
make sure we would never be found out. There was no
real danger of my conquests telling the guards because
they wanted sex as much as I did. But it was a rush thinking about the danger and risks involved. I learned how to
sneak around and plan out each conquest, using manipulative and conniving schemes to seduce them. I was tense

and constantly on guard, but the fear of getting caught was like a drug, adding excitement to my exploits and driving me on for more.

While I thought I was being clever, I suspect the guards knew more than they let on. Jail has a culture all its own, with drug use and sex going on under the veneer of prison rules and regulations. And while I dabbled in the sex culture, I stayed far away from the drug culture of the jail. I also stayed away from fights and tried my best to appear a model prisoner. This eventually paid off.

━━━

After five months in the LA County Jail, a guard came over to me while I was working. "Thompson," he said, "we're sending you off to Wayside to finish your time. You'll be leaving at the end of the week."

Although unexpected, this was welcome news. Wayside Honor Rancho Castaic Farm was a minimum-security facility out in the country. Inmates who proved themselves not to be troublemakers would often get moved there. At Wayside, everyone had a job, some in the fields, some in the commissary, others in janitorial services. There was space to move around, and inmates could go outside and enjoy the farm animals, trees, sky, and fresh air. Somehow, I knew God was answering the many prayers of my parents and their friends.

Once again, I was loaded onto a bus with a group of inmates, but this time the mood was lighter. We were heading into the country. As I watched cars whiz by and tall buildings disappear behind us, I became hopeful. Was

God giving me another chance? Although I still had six months to serve, I was ready to embrace the next phase with more confidence.

When the bus pulled into the new facility, I was relieved to see a large grassy area with picnic tables scattered under trees and inmates strolling about free of constraints. Even the orientation was different. A guard read out the rules, but no one shouted. He simply emphasized that Wayside was a minimum-security facility and that it was a privilege to be there, so don't mess up!

Wayside also had chapel every Sunday, and I sensed I needed to go. The service was formal—very different from the Pentecostal church I was raised in—but Christian. The chaplain was a simple man with a kind disposition. I came to like and trust him over the remaining months of my stay. Even though I was still far from God—rebellious and on the prowl for sex—God seemed to be drawing me there. The hymns and the Bible teachings resonated and felt like a refreshing drink of water.

Within the first few weeks of my stay at Wayside, I was placed into a typist position to complete forms for supplies and other daily business that transpired at the facility. I did my job well and was grateful I had something constructive to do. I felt valued by my supervising officer, who appreciated my work. "You're twice as fast as the other inmates we've had doing this job," he told me one day.

Another saving grace was the visits I received from my parents. While most inmates only had sporadic visitors, my parents came every weekend, giving me money so I could deposit it into my jail account. After catching me up on news from home, they would pray with me and encourage me that I was loved by them and by God.

As the end of my sentence neared, my parents brought along a girl named Judi when they visited. She was a member of their church youth group and looked up to my mother as a spiritual mentor. My mom had told Judi about me and said she was concerned I might go back to my old friends and old ways if I didn't make new connections with young people in the church. She asked Judi if she would like to come with them when they visited me at Wayside to start up a friendship. I will forever be grateful that Judi, a lovely, sweet eighteen-year-old girl, said yes. During my remaining time at Wayside, Judi and I became friends, and I looked forward to spending more time with her once I was released.

Even with my typing job and the weekly visits from my parents, my remaining sentence went by slowly. I found myself counting down the days until my release, but I also used the time to reflect on the mistakes I had made. Many nights I lay in my bunk pondering my life choices. At first, I condemned myself for being foolish and getting caught. But after an experience with God in one of the chapel services, I gained a deeper understanding of my rebellion and sin. I realized my actions and decisions were to blame, and I was responsible for my choices. In other words, I had deserved to get caught. In fact, I deserved a lot worse.

When the day finally came for my release, I waited to collect my personal items, thanking God for being with me and giving me the strength to persevere. I promised Him I would serve Him from then on. As I stripped off my prison clothes and put on my street clothes, I felt like a new man.

My parents were waiting when I walked out. What a welcome sight! Even so, there was a strangeness to it. The outside seemed almost foreign. Had I been gone that long? As much as I desired to embrace life away from jail, I felt like an outsider. It would take a while for me to become fully acclimated.

I climbed into the backseat of my parents' car and listened as they engaged in light conversation. I think they were trying to avoid the awkwardness of saying anything unpleasant. Even if I had wanted to, I wouldn't have been able to articulate what I was feeling. I just wanted to leave it all behind. My mom seemed to understand and never pushed me to talk.

Things were looking up. I had promised God, and I would become a new man. Little did I realize how long and twisting that road to change would be.

The Los Angeles County Jail used to be located on the top four floors of the old Los Angeles County Courthouse.

17

ONE STEP FORWARD,
FOUR STEPS BACK

When I was released from jail, I returned to my parents' home, determined to become the kind of man they would be proud of, a man who would never repeat his old mistakes. I was through with jail and the way of life that landed me there. This is where I started to become sick and tired of being sick and tired. Notice I said "started."

Determined to change, I recommitted my life to God and began going to church whenever there was a service. I became actively involved in the church youth and young adult group, and because I was older and had so much zeal for the Lord, I was asked to lead the youth group. Judi and I became close through this association, and we started spending time together. Mostly we shared a mutual love of music. She loved to sing almost as much as I did, and I started bringing my guitar to the youth meetings — a big hit with the teens. Judi and I began writing Christian music, practicing the songs for hours before introducing them to others in the group.

I invited her to join me in almost everything I did. She, being five years younger, felt privileged to be around my swirling frenzy of activity. Our small youth group grew from a few members to over fifty. It was the 1970s, and contemporary Christian music was just beginning to emerge. It became the vehicle we used to draw teenagers to Christ and away from drugs. We created Peace Unlimited, a nonprofit organization to reach young people, and began booking acts from all over the region to perform Christian concerts. Hundreds of youths were coming to these events.

All seemed to be going well, except for one thing—and it was a big thing. Although I was staying away from my former sins and doing things for God, my inner walk was floundering. My personal times with God were infrequent at best, and I never explored the root of my sin and rebellion. It was too painful. Because the Bible says, "Old things have passed away, behold, all things have become new,"[14] I didn't think there was anymore work to do. That is, I didn't think I needed to address my past or deal with my broken belief system and the memories that were hot-wired into my brain. This is how I avoided the pain. Because of this, the deep wounds from my childhood festered, and my relationship with God became stagnant. I was satisfied with doing things *for* Christ instead of being *in* Christ.

Everyone believed I had turned the corner—the youth group, my pastor, my parents, even Judi. She had fallen for

---

14   "Therefore if any man be in Christ, he is a new creature: old things are passed away; behold all things are become new" (2 Corinthians 5:17).

me, believing she had found a godly man to love her. She had no idea of the strongholds still clinging to my heart. To be honest, I had fooled myself as well. I knew Judi was in love with me, and I had fallen in love with her. She represented all that was good in my life. With her by my side, I was working for the kingdom of God, sharing with teens about the dangers of drugs, and watching them become free in Christ. Much like my relationship with Kathy back in high school, my relationship with Judi was pure and innocent. I was so focused on what we were doing together in Christ that I didn't think about sex or sexual things. But looking back, I realize I was living in denial. I didn't want to face my past or my broken relationship with my father.

Judi and I became inseparable whenever I was working to promote the youth ministry. I couldn't imagine going through life without her. I knew there was only one thing I could do to solve this problem, and I secretly planned out my proposal to her. She cried happy tears when I placed a ring on her finger.

My slide backward started rather innocuously. Our youth group ministry was growing with far more young people coming to our meetings than our church building could hold. When we outgrew the small room at the back of the church, we took over the main sanctuary on Tuesday nights. But I knew even this wouldn't hold us for long. I had big plans, and I needed a big building—a place where we could have large Christian concerts and invite young people from across the region.

I started looking for the perfect venue to buy, but this was more difficult than I had anticipated. When the location was perfect, the building was too small. When the building was large enough, it was in a terrible location.

Then I discovered a large building that had once been a bowling alley on some property along the Pacific Coast Highway. It had a beautiful view of the ocean to the west and the coastal mountains to the east, and it had been vacant for several years. It seemed perfect, and I knew it must be God's will that we would have it—no matter what the cost. I joyfully declared the good news to the youth group and claimed it in prayer for our youth ministry. No hurdles could stand in the way of God's will, I told them. This building was going to be our new home. We just needed to believe this was what God wanted and trust Him to provide it.

Sitting on prime real estate, the building was selling for an enormous sum of money. Maintaining the property and paying the taxes would also be a huge month-to-month expense. But I believed God would take care of all those details and provide the way for us to have it.

However, the money never came, and the building was eventually sold to another buyer. When I saw the "sold" sign go up, it was like a cold dagger went through my heart. I was disappointed and embarrassed over what I had proclaimed in faith to the youth. *How could God do this to me?* I silently raged.

This wedge of disappointment grew deeper into my thought process. I couldn't shake it, and because I wasn't accountable and open with those I was close to, I didn't talk to anyone about it. Instead, I took offense against God. "Really, God? Really? After all I've been through? You couldn't do this one thing for me? Instead, you make me look like a fool to everyone!"

Ironically, another Christian church purchased the old bowling alley, but this felt like a slap in the face to me. I didn't even consider meeting with the leadership of that church to see if we could work together. I was so convinced that God had wanted Peace Unlimited to own the building, I never thought God might have a different plan.

I silently raged against God, fueling fires of rebellion. At first, I tried to ignore the rebellious thoughts and continued going through the motions of being the youth leader. But it didn't take long for my anger to consume and affect everything I did and everyone I spent time with. Instead of doing things for God, I began spending most of my time with old friends who enjoyed smoking pot and taking drugs. In no time, I joined them in their alcohol and drug binges. I also began making routine visits to public toilets for gay sex.

It didn't take long for the pastor to catch on. When he questioned me about my attitude and behavior, my response was lackluster. He asked me to resign as the youth leader, and I was happy to oblige.

And then there was Judi. Even she didn't get away unscathed. Still devoted to me, she tagged along on some of my drug-induced adventures. She was so young and naïve, watching in horror as the man she loved was losing his compass and his senses. Still, she stayed with me, hoping that this was just a phase and that I would soon get my life back in order. She had no idea how deep the pit of my sins went and how fiercely they held me.

I finally had a moment of sanity and realized I was pulling Judi into something she didn't deserve, and so I broke off our engagement. Judi's gaze penetrated mine. Anger, hurt, confusion—all seemed to be screaming from her eyes. I wished I could run and hide—avoid this painful moment. How could I do this to her? Didn't I love her?

"I don't understand," she finally said, emotions choking her voice so that it was barely audible. "I thought you loved me."

She looked down at the ring I had given her, removed it from her finger, and handed it back to me. It was my promise that I loved her above everyone else. But it had all been a promise made in haste—a selfish whim on my part, not understanding how much pull the underbelly of my passions still had on me. How did their tentacles grip me once again, pulling me away from God and away from Judi?

She was heartbroken, and so was I. She told me years later that she eventually came to terms with it, realizing I couldn't change because I didn't want to.

The snake was back, and this time it appeared he wasn't going to let me go.

A few months after our breakup, I went on an all-night, drug-induced, sex-orgy binge. When I finally pulled up outside my parents' house the next morning, Judi was standing at the curb—anger and pain searing her expression.

"Where have you been?" she demanded, her voice louder and sharper than I had ever heard it before.

I was annoyed and hungover. "What?"

"We've been trying to reach you all night. Your mom called me to see if I had the phone numbers of your friends. We couldn't find you anywhere."

Her comment jarred me. Something was wrong. "What's going on?" I asked.

"Your father is dead," she blurted out. "He had a heart attack."

*Judi and I were first engaged
in the early '70s.*

Judi in 1971.

18

THE FUNERAL

I added my father's death to a long list of excuses for my bad behavior. He was seventy years old when his heart gave out; I was twenty-five. No one saw it coming, but everyone blamed me. At least that's what I thought. Looking back, I know this was my shame talking. All I knew was that I had broken his heart many times, and I believed I was a constant disappointment to him.

In the days after his passing, I had this overwhelming sense of loss and dejection. I had been on an all-night binge while my father struggled for his life—so typical of my uncaring and self-centered ways. How many times had my parents provided a safety net for me and welcomed me back home when I needed them, knowing full well that I had been up to no good? And how did I thank them? How did I show my appreciation?

It was too late for my father. He was dead, and he was never coming back. There would be no more chances to make things right, and this didn't seem fair. We were never able to talk, and I felt robbed of a close relationship with him. Ever since the day I was molested by Pat at the age of eleven, I believed my father was ashamed of me. Now I would never find out why things had gone the way they had.

My poor mother had been the one to find him. I couldn't pour my heart out to her because she was walking around in a gloomy haze. I had never seen her like this. Brian, always the dutiful son, hardly left her side. The two of them became very close during this time, and I began to resent my brother for this.

Judi came over from time to time the week after my dad passed, but she wasn't there for me. She was there for my mom. I couldn't talk to her; I had burned that bridge when I broke our engagement.

I isolated myself from everyone, deeply sad yet unable to grieve with those I loved most. Part of this was due to my guilty conscience, and the other part was due to fear. I didn't want to see their faces blaming me for what had happened.

I don't remember much about the funeral service, except that the church was packed with people. My parents had a lot of friends, and hundreds came to pay their respects. When it was time for the funeral procession, I was unaware of any plans about who should ride with whom. I followed Brian and my mother out of the church and watched as Brian escorted Mom to his car. No one invited me to join them, so I walked back to my car, which was at the far end of the parking lot. By the time I made it to the procession, I was about ten cars back from the hearse—nowhere near my brother's car or even the extended family.

They don't want me with them, I thought. *They're blaming me for this.*

My mind churned in self-pity. I was angry at my mother, my brother, my father, and pretty much everyone who had attended the funeral. I tried to see over the cars to the hearse, but I couldn't see it. So many years had gone by with no closeness between me and my father. I was an outcast in my own family. Just like this procession—stuck at the back, away from everyone. Why had my dad made me feel so ashamed when I was only eleven? Why hadn't he taken me in his arms and told me it was okay? Why hadn't he told me it wasn't my fault? Instead, I felt he had blamed me. I assumed he was ashamed of me—his queer, strange son. Not like Brian. Never like Brian.

When I finally reached the cemetery, I slammed my car door and headed directly over to Brian and my mom. Brian saw me coming and must have sensed something was wrong because he immediately started heading my way.

"Wynn," he called out. "We're—"

"Of course," I interrupted, marching up to him. "Why the hell was I not riding in the family car? Are you ashamed of me? Ashamed that I'm part of this family? Well, guess what? I *am* part of this family!"

"Wynn," Brian said in a hushed whisper. "Calm down—"

"I was ten cars back, Brian. Ten!" I held both hands up so that he could count all ten fingers.

Poor Brian was doing his best to quiet my anger, but it wasn't working. I suddenly realized everyone was looking at me, so I stormed away. *I need to cool off,* I told myself, taking in deep breaths as I walked among the headstones at the far end of the cemetery. Eventually, I made my way back to the service and watched while the minister said the final prayer. Then I walked back to my car.

Blowing up at my brother during my father's burial is something I've had to live with. I wish I could take it back, but like all the other mistakes I've made, I can only learn from it.

19

THE RAT RACE

When a friend suggested I apply for a sales position at a beer distribution company, I jumped at the chance to start making some real money. I was hired and tasked with promoting the product at different venues throughout the Hollywood and Beverly Hills area. The job included lots of driving, lots of friendly conversations, and lots of drinking — all of which I was good at. I was a tireless worker and became one of the top sales reps in the company. Unfortunately, I was also a tireless player, spending my nights in drug-indulged orgies after working sixteen-hour days. I took speed to stay awake, which was especially needed since I lived near the coast and drove the freeways into the heart of LA every day. I can't tell you how many times I drove home drunk and full of drugs, yet I never got into an accident, and I was never pulled over.

My same-sex exploits during this time were tireless. At one point, I had two lovers at the same time. Eventually, I fell hard for a man seven years younger than me. I was so entranced by him that I became obsessed and constantly worried that he would leave me—something he did often. Each time he left, I would fall into a tailspin of depression and anxiety. Then he would come back, only to put me through the same torment again. Finally, he decided he didn't want to be gay anymore and left me for a woman. When this happened, I became an emotional wreck—addicted to work, addicted to alcohol, addicted to sex, addicted to drugs, and completely deprived of sleep. Everything caught up with me the day I nearly passed out at work while talking to a client. That's when I decided to take a week off—something I rarely did—and make a doctor's appointment.

I sat, pale and trembling, on the edge of the patient table, watching the doctor read from the clipboard in his hands. A middle-aged man with dark glasses and thinning hair, he seemed puzzled, shaking his head as he read. Finally, he looked up.

"You say you're . . ." he started, then glanced down at the clipboard, "thirty-two?"

I nodded, fearing the worst but hoping for better. My energy level was sapped, and I was constantly shaking.

"Mr. Thompson, you're in terrible health—especially for a thirty-two-year-old," he said. "I don't know what you've been doing, but I suspect drugs and alcohol—and lots of it."

Was that a question? He looked like he was waiting for an answer. I nodded.

"How well do you sleep?"

Sleep? Now there was a thought. For the past seven years, I was lucky to get two hours a night.

The doctor seemed to read my mind. "You've been abusing your body for a long time. That's obvious," he said, disgust evident in his tone. "Frankly, I suspect if you don't get out of LA—and soon—you're going to be carried out."

His words felt like an omen. Did I want to die like an old man when I was still young?

Working for the beer distributor.

PART THREE

Redemption

20

A T U R N I N G P O I N T

I knew the doctor was right. My lifestyle was killing me, and the only chance I had was to leave it all behind. But where would I go? Years earlier, my brother had transferred to the small town of Bishop in northeast California, and my mother had soon followed him up there. Bishop had a population of twelve hundred in the early '80s. It sits at the base of the Sierra Nevadas on the way to Mammoth Mountain, a ski mecca for those living in Southern California. It seemed like the perfect answer to my dilemma. I took trips from LA to Bishop on the weekends to investigate the area, and within a short time, I found an affordable mobile home and started the mortgage paperwork. Because I was desperate to leave LA, I quit my job six months before I was eligible to withdraw from retirement without being penalized by taxes, sold most of my things, and bought a red Mustang.

It was 1981, and the AIDS epidemic had just started spreading in Hollywood. Moving to Bishop probably saved my life. It was an enormous change of pace. I lived with my two cockapoos in a quiet neighborhood between my mother's upscale mobile home park and the housing development where my brother and his family lived.

Eventually, my lover's relationship with the woman he was dating ended, and he followed me up to Bishop. Neither he nor I worked the first year we were there. Instead, I supported us with my disability check and what was left from my retirement fund. Being able to visit with my mother during this time meant the world to me. She was always a rock of stability in my life, so in love with the Lord and still playing the piano in worship at her church. Living in Bishop also allowed me to become closer to Brian, his wife, and their two sons. When I wasn't visiting family, I spent my days sitting at home watching movies or just hanging out with my roommate. Although I knew he was using me to have a free place to live, I didn't care because he kept me company, and I was still emotionally attached to him.

I was also still drinking alcohol and smoking pot at this time, but I was drinking much less and had completely stopped using speed. For the most part, life was quiet, and I was slowly regaining my health.

⸺

After a year of my living on disability, Brian came over with a proposal. He had volunteered with a group of community leaders to bring a public television station to Bishop and needed some help providing programming to fill in space during a telethon. Because of my background in the entertainment industry, he figured I might know something about it. I didn't, but I needed a change of pace and gladly took him up on the offer.

The station only had one video camera, so I used that and my personal video camera to tape live performances of music groups around town. I taped from two different angles with the two cameras, which allowed me to edit the recordings so that it appeared the groups were being taped by a camera crew switching back and forth from different angles. I had no experience with any of this, but I had seen camera crews operate on sets in Hollywood.

The programming was shown during the telethon and was well received. After this, a poet named Eva Pool-Gilson contacted me about helping her produce *Art Break*, a show on the local cable channel that featured local artists. She received grant money to pay for everything we needed. I worked the cameras and did the editing, while she wrote the scripts and conducted the interviews. We did twelve shows per season for two seasons.

Eventually, this matriculated into me being invited to create and run a live ninety-minute TV show called *Daybreak*. I was also asked to film pieces for the local news station. Because I never wrote, directed, shot, or hosted a TV show before, I had to make it up as I went along. I began developing ideas for interviews and segments to fill the live portions of the ninety minutes allotted to me. One fantastic boon was when Rebecca Cobb came by the studio and asked if she could help with the morning show. She made a fabulous cohost, contributing to the popularity of the show with her talent, ideas, and personality. When Rebecca moved to Southern California, she was replaced by cohosts Teri Dee and Lynn Connor. Both women were instrumental in helping me with *School Report*, a successful segment featuring different teachers and students every month. School district administrators would select the teacher, and we would conduct the interviews at the school before filming the students doing their assignments. Parents loved it because they could tune in and see their kids on TV.

 ⁓

Although I was becoming well known and liked around town, I still felt empty and unhappy. My hidden sins haunted me—even after the hedonism was gone. In short, my life seemed pointless. My ex-lover had moved back to LA, and I was living alone with my dogs again. I remember waking up one morning in 1985, trudging over to the bathroom, and staring at my thirty-nine-year-old face in the mirror. I was disheartened. Being gay is for the young and beautiful, and I wasn't getting any younger. The last thing I wanted to be was an old gay man. And yet that's exactly where I was heading.

I thought about a time when I was selling beer to the bars and clubs around Hollywood and walked into a gay bar just off Hollywood Boulevard. At first, I couldn't see anything because it was so dark inside. But as my vision adjusted, I saw a long, narrow, smoke-filled room. On the left was a tatty wooden bar with three old gay men drinking and smoking. In the back were about five or six tables with one man sitting alone. All of them were at least sixty, possibly older. There was no laughter, no life. It was very depressing and made me feel sad. *How pathetic,* I thought. *I never want to be like this when I'm that old.*

My years in Bishop had mellowed me, making me realize there was something greater than city life and the constant demand for pleasure. Leaving LA, the drug culture, and the rat race helped, but it wasn't enough. I wanted out of the gay lifestyle and everything it stood for. It was that simple. I had finally come to the point where I really was sick and tired of being sick and tired. I was at a breaking point, and something had to change.

There was only one answer, and I knew it was Jesus. Had He really waited for me all these years to come to Him? In my mind, I saw Him hanging, bloody and beaten on the cross, taking the punishment for my sins so that I could live in His righteousness. I didn't deserve it, and yet I knew He offered it anyway because He loved me. Would I finally accept it?

Slowly, I got down on my knees and laid my heart before Him. "Lord," I prayed, "You know where I've been, what I've been doing. You know me. And I'm so very sorry. Please help me. I can't make it without You. Help me to become a new creation. I promise to follow You, but I need Your help. I can't do this without You."

For the first time, I had come to the point of godly sorrow and true repentance.

Mom and me at her new home in Bishop, California, late '70s.

Mom in 1981.

Brian, Kay, and me, Bishop.

Filming at the Mule Days Parade in Bishop.

Filming "School Report" in one of the classrooms.

Rebecca, my cohost, on my TV show Daybreak.

21

THE BATTLE BEGINS

A twenty-two-year-old stud stood at my door—muscular body, tanned skin, blond hair. I was in my robe, a half-filled coffee mug in my hand. It was 9 a.m.

I almost couldn't believe it when I answered the door and this young, gorgeous guy greeted me. I hadn't seen him in several months. I had only connected with him twice before, and that was over a year ago. Would I like to join him for some fun down by the river? I couldn't believe *he* was asking *me*. I mean, this guy had never come on to me before. It had always been me who approached him. The thrill of being pursued like this was almost irresistible. And yet . . . there was another voice—a very soft voice— whispering, *You made a promise.*

But how could I resist *him*? Surely one more time wouldn't make any difference.

The inner voice continued to pierce my conscience. How could I explain to this guy that I had given my life to God? That I had promised God I would no longer use my body this way? The words to explain this were not even in my vocabulary. I hemmed and hawed, trying to make excuses as we conversed. Then I noticed something strange. The foul language coming from the young man's lips, the way he spoke it out as a matter of course, had been the way I ordinarily spoke as well. But I wasn't talking this way now. No swear words were coming out of my mouth.

Oh my God, I thought. *I really am different!*

Emboldened by this thought, I stood my ground. After twenty minutes, the young man finally gave up. "Well," he said, "I'll be down there if you change your mind."

After closing the door, I leaned against it and said an audible prayer of thanksgiving.

What a victory! Although I was still very tempted to fall back into my old patterns of sin, God was teaching me how to flex my "no" muscle.

This was the first real victory over my flesh I had ever experienced, and it wouldn't be the last. But along with the victories, there would also be some defeats.

I had just signed up for a battle, and I wasn't sure if I had it in me to win.

~

Because I was uncertain about whether I could stay the course,[15] I didn't rush right over to my mom's house with the news about my recommitment to Christ. I approached things a lot more stealthily. Like a small child getting into a cold swimming pool one toe at a time, I eased into it by first attending my mom's church. My mom, now in her seventies, still played piano during the worship portion of

---

15   A term used in Christianity that means continuing to follow God in all circumstances.

the service. After finishing, she sat in the front row. When I first started attending, I sat in the very back, where all the other "sinners" usually sat. I knew I belonged by her side, but it took me a while to get there. Each Sunday, I moved up a row until I was finally sitting with my mom about six weeks later. Seeing me in church again brought such joy to her. She had never stopped praying for me, and she eagerly told everyone about my recommitment.

I knew I had to take God seriously if I was going to continue in the faith. I read His Word daily and desired to live in righteousness before Him. The alcohol and marijuana were easy to give up, but my sex addiction was a battle. I often fell back into viewing pornography and then cried out to God for forgiveness. This became a pattern, and it wasn't healthy. I realized if I was ever going to beat this addiction, I would need some outside help. Fortunately, my pastor knew of an assistant pastor at Jack Hayford's church in Van Nuys who came out of a similar sexual addiction. My pastor scheduled an appointment for me to talk with this man over the phone. The call was long distance, and my pastor graciously let me use the phone in his church office. The assistant pastor from Van Nuys quietly listened as I told him my story. It was such a relief to unload on someone who had experienced the same kinds of struggles. When I finished, he asked me a simple question: "Have you cleaned house?"

Missing the metaphor completely, I said, "Um . . . I've vacuumed and washed my dishes."

There was a short pause on the other end of the line.

Then: "You know what I mean. Have you gotten rid of your stash?"

"My stash?"

"The porn," he said bluntly. "And all gifts from your past life and lovers—anything that connects you with your past brokenness."

I didn't answer right away. How did he know about my stash of porn that I had collected over the years? Not to mention the pictures and movies I had taken of past conquests?

I finally admitted that I hadn't.

"Get rid of it—all of it," he said. "You've got to clean house, or you will never be free of it."

I nodded, but of course he couldn't see me.

"Are you serious about this?" he asked.

I exhaled. "Yes."

～

That phone call took only fifteen minutes, but it was the start of a life-changing process. I knew what I had to do and was determined to show both God and me that I meant business. Although it was a summer afternoon, I fired up the woodstove in my living room and hauled out a large box filled with photographs, greeting cards from past lovers, and pornographic videotapes. It was a warm day, and the heat from the stove made the temperature inside almost unbearable. I opened the door to the woodstove, feeling the heat against my face. Then I lifted out one picture at a time, turning each over face up so I could get a last look before feeding it into the fire.

I thought of Lot's wife looking back at Sodom[16] as it was being destroyed. She was turned into a pillar of salt. *Maybe the same thing will happen to me.* Beads of sweat rolled down my face as each photo was consumed by flames, turning from orange to red to blue. A burning sensation seared through my conscience as each one shriveled into black ash. Something was happening in the spiritual realm, and the physical pain was incredible. Every muscle in my body cringed and tightened as if the sinews were being ripped from the bones. I didn't realize it at the time, but I now understand I was undergoing self-deliverance, and the demons were fighting to stay right where they were.

Because the videotapes were plastic and couldn't be burned, I put each one in the tape player, turned on my TV, and recorded over them. This took several hours, but I was so focused on what I was doing that I didn't pay attention to what was being recorded. After each video was rerecorded, I angrily broke them apart with a hammer and cut up the tape so that there would be no possibility of anything ever being found or discovered.

I was finally finished around 3 a.m.—my former life turned to plastic shards and ash. In exhaustion, I collapsed on the carpet and wept. Huge waves of pain and regret were flowing out of me. I was overcome with godly sorrow and experiencing the depths of brokenness before my Savior. Then I felt Jesus lifting me with His nail-scarred hands from the cesspool that had been my life. A deep and surreal joy filled me—so much so that I rushed out into the

---

16   This comes from the story of the destruction of Sodom and Gomorrah in Genesis 19.

street and whispered, "I'm free." The early-morning sky was dark and cool, but my heart was filled with light and joy. I was well on my way to becoming a new creation in Christ. My old life was dead. New things were waiting!

I said a short prayer of thanksgiving to God for His goodness, love, and mercy before going to bed. Then, engulfed in peace, I faded off to sleep.

22

TRIALS, TRIBULATIONS, AND TEMPTATIONS

I wish I could say there was smooth sailing from then on, but Satan doesn't give up so easily. My next temptation completely blindsided me—mainly because it came from a woman. She was a redhead who ran a radio program in town. From out of nowhere, she started giving me compliments and sending me flirtatious signals such as a touch on the shoulder or a caress on the hand. Gifts from her started appearing on my desk at work or on my front porch. I loved the attention and asked her to join me for dinner one night. In almost no time, we were sleeping together.

The sexual sin I thought I had burned to ashes had found a new window to climb through. I felt dirty, and my old companion—shame—came back with a vengeance. I knew what I was doing was wrong. I didn't even love this woman, nor did she love me. She was using me like a hired gigolo for her sexual gratification, and I felt miserable. I could no longer face God nor my brothers and sisters in Christ. I knew if I didn't do something fast, I would drift back into my old addictions. After struggling for several weeks in indecision, I finally broke off the relationship and cried out to God for forgiveness.

God used this failure to teach me a very important lesson: My sexual addiction was not a battle I could win on my own. I needed God's help, and I wouldn't get it by being just a Sunday-only Christian. I needed to immerse myself in His Word and be at church or with other believers at every opportunity. Even my work needed to bring glory to God, and I began featuring Christian music artists on my show and interviewing different people in ministries around town.

I was beginning to feel like God was using me for His purposes.

Everything seemed to be going along smoothly until Mom's health started to rapidly decline in 1991. She went from playing piano at church to being so weak she couldn't leave her house on some days. Brian, his wife, Kay, and I took turns caring for her when she was too weak to function well. The last thing we wanted was for her to live in a nursing home. My mom had always been such a strong woman—a real lady. She was used to being the helper, not the one needing help. But now she was reduced to a mere shell of her former self, needing us to cook for her, clean up after her, bathe her, put her to bed—everything. It broke our hearts.

Even so, I wouldn't erase the experience I had during the final years of my mother's life. Although her body was failing, her mind was alert, and the walls of communication that had never been breached before were now falling down. We spent hours talking about things we had never discussed before, and it didn't take long for the secrets to come out. When I told her about the four teenage boys who had raped me at age six, she wept and reached her thin arms out to embrace me.

"I am so, so sorry," she said. "I had no idea. I'm sorry I wasn't able to protect you and you didn't feel you could tell us."

Exposing my dark secrets through our open communication had a profound effect on me. It was the beginning of a deeper healing journey. My mom appreciated knowing the truth about me as well because it helped her to understand why I had made some of the choices in my life. She wanted to know everything and had lots of questions.

"I've always wanted to talk to you about what happened with Pat," Mom said one day. "I should never have let you go over to her house like that. It was all my fault."

I couldn't believe what I was hearing. "It was Pat's fault, Mom. It wasn't your fault," I said. "I've never blamed you. You had no idea what Pat was going to do. But I always felt like Dad blamed me for what happened. Like he was ashamed of me from then on."

Mom shook her head. "You're wrong, Wynn. Your father always blamed himself for what happened. He carried that weight around for decades. He longed to fix the damage, but he didn't know how. And I think that's what frustrated him."

"Then why didn't he say something?" I asked. "Why did he make me feel like he didn't love me because of the way I was?"

"Your dad loved you more than you could ever imagine," she said, tears in her eyes. "He just didn't know how to express it very well."

I was shocked. Was this true? I was about to argue, but then I thought about all the times my father had let me come home and live with them after I was an adult. He had never given up on me. Even when he knew I was deeply lost and actively pursuing a sinful lifestyle, he kept his door open and was there to help pick me up when I fell. All this time, I thought it had only been because of my mother's influence. But now I realized my dad did it because he loved and cared about me. He had never stopped loving me. He had longed to have a close father-son bond with me—probably even more than I longed to have it with him. All my life, I had believed a lie. My dad was *not* ashamed of me. He had not been disappointed in me. Why had I gone through all that rebellion, anger, and rage? What a waste of time! If only I had known the truth.

Another healing process started that day. I knew it would take some time to fully process, but what a reunion will take place when I see my dad again in eternity!

Mom at her favorite place, the piano.

At my editing desk at the new channel 12 TV station, 1989.

23

THE RECKONING

Not long after this, the enemy threw a wildcard my way. It started with a phone call.

"This is the sheriff, Wynn," the voice said. "You need to come to the station right away. It's important."

My mind raced as I hung up. Had I done something illegal? Unethical? I couldn't think of anything.

Sheriff Mike was sitting behind his desk when I walked in. He motioned for me to take a seat, and I timidly complied. I had interviewed Mike on my TV show over the years, and we had a good relationship. I had never seen him act so official before.

"Is something wrong?" I asked.

"You could say that," he said. "Were you aware that, as a felony sex offender, you are required to register with the court whenever you move?"

Sex offender? Where did this information come from? I was speechless. Then it hit me. A month before, the TV station where I worked had hired two new journalists who were young and fresh out of media school. These new recruits asked if they could apply for press passes so they could gain free access to events. Although press passes had never been necessary before, I applied for one as well to show my support. The press pass application process included a background check, but my past seemed so far behind me that I didn't even think about my criminal record coming up.

I tried to recall what the judge had told me more than twenty years earlier when I was convicted of felony drug and sex charges. Hadn't the sex offender status been rescinded when they lowered my sentence? Or was that just wishful thinking?

"I believe that was waived by the judge. I don't think I'm required to register," I said. "It happened so long ago."

The sheriff thumbed through the papers on his desk. "I don't see any indication of that here. Do you have it in writing somewhere?"

"I think so. Can I go home to look for it?"

The sheriff nodded. "Call me as soon as you find it. You have until ten tomorrow morning."

I never did find the waiver. I'm fairly certain it was only wishful thinking on my part. After scouring my mobile home in every possible drawer and container, I called my lawyer. "You'd better go back and turn yourself in," she said. "Maybe they'll go easy on you."

When I walked back into the station, the deputies—I knew them both by name—politely led me through the booking process. Their kind treatment was so different from the way I had been treated by the police when I was a boy and young man.

I was immediately released to await my court hearing. Because Bishop is a small town and I was a TV personality, my arrest was considered big news. The newspaper and radio station were competitors of the television station where I worked, so reporters covered every detail of the court proceedings. My criminal record became front-page news and the subject of several radio broadcasts. There was no place for me to hide. I sought solace from my family, my pastor, and four older women from my church, who prayed for me every day.

A month later, my brother, Brian, dropped me off at the jail where I would be serving out my three-month sentence. He embraced me and told me he was very sorry.

I was touched by his support. Brian knew I was a different man.

And so did God.

24

DARKEST BEFORE DAWN

The hardest part about being back in jail wasn't that I had lost my job or my reputation. It was the haunting memory of my mother in tears as I said goodbye.

"I don't understand why God would do this to you," she had said, looking so small and frail in the large overstuffed chair next to the window in her living room.

I tried to be strong for her—putting on a brave face before I left to do my time—but the sight of her sad face and hearing her exasperation was alarming. Her thin frame heaved as tears streamed down her face. "You have changed so much," she cried. "You have been doing such wonderful things!"

This was so unlike her. She had experienced great heartache in her life, not only because of what I had put her through but also from her early years growing up with an abusive and alcoholic father. But God had worked all that together for His glory, building in her a strength of character and unshakable faith that I had never seen waver—until now.

Although I was deeply touched by her support, I hated thinking of her this way. What if she died while I was still incarcerated? She had been so weak when I left, and her frailty was taking its toll on her emotional well-being. I longed to be there for her, not rotting away in this jail.

"Oh, God," I prayed, "please don't take Mom home before I can see her again. I don't know if I could handle that."

I was comforted by Brian and Kay, who supported and encouraged me throughout this ordeal. I felt terrible about leaving them with the full burden of Mom's caretaking. Mom was becoming so weak, and having one less person to share the load would be hard on them. A few weeks after I was booked into jail, her condition became so poor that Brian was forced to find a nursing home where she could receive twenty-four-hour care. Unfortunately, the closest affordable facility was in Lone Pine, an hour's distance from Bishop.

Thoughts of my family's struggle and my inability to help sent me to God's throne daily. *Haven't I turned my life around?* I cried out silently to God. *Haven't I been faithful to do what I could to incorporate You into every area of my life, even at work?*

I was learning the hard way that sin has consequences — even after we turn back to God. But He also had another purpose for this trial, something I would need in my future walk with Him.

I thought about a visiting minister who had preached at our church before I was to begin my sentence. In the middle of his sermon, he had looked out over the congregation and set his eyes on my face.

"You, sitting right there in the plaid shirt," he said. "God wants you to know He will be with you. You may be going through the flames, but you're going to come out on the other side without even the smell of smoke on you."

This clear reference to Meshach, Shadrach, and Abednego from the book of Daniel[17] encouraged me. God knew what I was going through, and He wouldn't abandon me. This was the last time Mom had been physically able to attend church, and I took comfort that she had been there to hear it.

Another encouragement came from my pastor's wife, who called me a few days before I had to leave for jail. I had been in a deep depression for three days, feeling a bit like Job in Job chapter three. She reminded me that God had a purpose for my life, and she relayed a story from her youth that showed how God had used a painful experience to grow her faith in ways she could never have imagined.

"Don't worry about understanding it all now," she said. "Just keep tender before Him through it and trust Him. Eventually, you'll understand what you need to understand. The important thing is that you see this as an opportunity to grow closer to Him."

And then there was Ida, a friend of my mother's and a widow who went to our church. White-haired and energetic, Ida didn't let her advanced years stop her from visiting me every week while I was in jail. This was no easy task

---

17   Daniel 3.

for a woman in her seventies because the jail was a forty-five-minute drive from Bishop. Ida became my connection to the outside world. She brought news of my mother and became a spiritual mentor and prayer partner. Her cheery attitude was a beacon of light in the dark atmosphere of the jail.

In the same way, she was paying regular visits to my mom in Lone Pine, bringing her news about how I was doing. Ida's visits were like a balm of ointment on my aching heart.

Through Ida's friendship, my family's emotional support, and the words of encouragement and practical help from others, God was showing me His faithfulness. My three-month sentence was reduced to two months, and before I knew it, I was being released from jail and riding home with Ida.

As I walked into my mobile home, I breathed in the familiar smell. My two loyal cockapoos ran up, wagging their tails and yelping. My brother had taken care of them while I was away and dropped them off at my house that morning before he went to work. It was so good to be back. But now what? I had no job, and the media had exposed the dark side of my former life. How could I face the town again? Still, Mom was in a nursing home. There was no running away from that. I decided to focus on first things first: spend as much time as possible with Mom before she passed. The rest would have to wait.

It's amazing how God had orchestrated things in my life beforehand to prepare me for what was happening now. Although I had no job, I also had no debt. And this didn't happen by accident. A few years earlier, I had been in terrible financial straits after forming my own production company. Because I was unskilled in running my own business, I had hired an accountant to handle my books and all my taxes. Everything had gone smoothly with this arrangement the first year, but then the firm had failed to pay my taxes the following several years, and I had not even noticed when the statements and bills stopped coming. It wasn't until I received a notice of back taxes due to the IRS that I realized what a mess I was in. I was panic-stricken, unable to comprehend how I would pay the IRS the amount that was due.

My rescuer came in the form of a woman in her forties—a friend of a friend named Ione Reget. Ione was a certified public accountant, and she immediately took charge of the situation. She put me on a budget, with tight controls on my spending. Then she worked through my debt and managed to settle the amount owed to the IRS. Within a few years, I was debt-free and had a growing savings account. Things were going so well that Ione told me, "You can buy that car you want so badly now."

That's how I was able to purchase a new 1990 Ford Thunderbird.

How could I have foreseen I would lose my job and need every penny of that savings to survive now? I was the last person in the world who would have planned for something like that. And yet God knew and had taken care of it before everything fell apart.

God also provided me with a group of lady friends who served as an anchor of support. Ida was always there with a listening ear and a kind word. But she was also very honest and unafraid to speak hard truths into my life. Ida introduced me to her group of lady friends from our church—three other widows in their seventies who gathered several nights a week for dinner and board games. They accepted me into their group like a gaggle of hens rescuing a lost chick and became my closest confidants.

Ida's friends included Velma, the wife of the founding pastor of our church; Ione Longest; and Dorothy. Velma lived with Ida in the parsonage next to the church. She was a white-haired ball of energy who loved life and, except for my mom, was the most hospitable person I've ever known. She cooked dinner for us almost every night of the week. And, boy, could she cook!

Ione Longest, my mom's childhood friend, had experienced a lot of pain and sorrow in her life. She and my mom had lost touch over the years, but they had providentially chanced upon one another in Bishop—and this was before the internet! The frailest and shortest of the group, Ione was kind and considerate, but she also had a peppery streak and loved to tease. Whenever she won at Aggravation or Uno, she'd celebrate by rubbing her victory into the faces of the losers. I was her favorite target during these shenanigans—a clear indication she liked me.

Dorothy was the tallest of the four ladies, with mixed white, gray, and brown hair. She could be a bit cantankerous, but she was willing to concede when appropriate.

She loved to win at games and would let loose deep belly laughs during our playful discourse. When I first started coming over for their gatherings, Dorothy seemed a bit perturbed by my intrusion. But I eventually won her over, and she became one of my greatest cheerleaders.

Fellowshipping with these women through shared meals, encouragement, games—I have never played so many board games in my entire life!—and laughter was like ointment to my aching heart. It not only helped to sustain me, but it also helped me to thrive when I could have easily floundered in despair.

One night after chiding me for losing at the card game Uno, Ida looked sideways at the other ladies and then disappeared into the kitchen. She returned with a flier in her hand and gave it to me.

"What's this?" I asked, scanning the bold heading at the top.

"Have you ever heard of YWAM?" she asked, her eyes sparkling.

With Mom in front of my mobile home in Bishop.

With my senior confidants:
Ida, Ione, Dorothy, and Velma, 1992.

Winning at Aggravation, much to the chagrin of my cohorts.

With Ida, 1997.

Ida in Trafalgar Square, London, England, 1997.

PART FOUR

Service

25

YWAM

YWAM stands for Youth with a Mission, a proven global mission organization. It was 1992, and I was in my forties—hardly a youth. But for some reason, I felt a tug from the Holy Spirit to go with Ida to the YWAM meeting advertised on the flier she had given me.

There was a YWAM training and retreat center in the mountains, about forty-five minutes away from Bishop, but this event was at a school auditorium in town. A YWAM schoolteacher and former missionary was coming to speak at the event. There were about forty people in attendance as Ida and I found our seats. Then a man with an acoustic guitar began leading worship. There were no special effects, no fancy sound systems, no band. Just people who loved the Lord singing their hearts out in humble surrender. I could sense the Spirit of God's presence in the room.

Afterward, a tall, angular man looking to be in his thirties approached the podium. "Thank you for coming," he said. "What an intimate time of worship! Isn't God wonderful?"

Several in the audience nodded.

"Well, I have a feeling that tonight is going to be even more amazing than we expected. Here's the thing: Our speaker wasn't able to make it due to sickness. But how many here know that God has a way of changing our plans? He's interrupted us tonight for a reason, and that's a good thing. Amen?"

"Amen!" A man in the back row boomed out.

"So instead of listening to a speaker, we're going to teach you how to hear the voice of God. Are you up for that?"

"Amen!" A few more people answered.

"Then lean in, because what you're going to learn tonight will change the way you pray forever."

They brought out a long strip of newsprint and pinned it up on the back wall. The teacher divided the audience into four groups of ten, and one person from each group was chosen to be a scribe. The groups were instructed to be quiet before the Lord, inviting the Holy Spirit to speak to them. After about five minutes in silence, the scribes were to ask their groups about what they heard or saw from God and then write those things down on a notepad.

Ida and I joined one of the groups, and people began to pray silently. The presence of the Holy Spirit was evident, and we were expectant. After silently listening and praying for several minutes, our group began to share what the Lord had shown them. The young lady who served as our scribe busily jotted everything down.

"Okay," the teacher said, "let's have the scribes come up."

One by one, the four scribes read their notes to the leader, who wrote them up on the newsprint for everyone to see. When all were finished, the newsprint was filled with words and scribbled pictures.

"Now let's make some connections," the teacher said, taking a black marker and standing with his back to the audience as he studied the board. He began circling common phrases and pictures. The result was incredible. Although there were four separate groups, common threads ran through all the notes. Once the common threads were spotted and connected, we began praying as one large group, focusing on those specific topics. I had never experienced such a powerful time of intercessory prayer.[18]

When we were finished, the teacher explained that these prayer threads would be recorded in a master book and sent out to all the YWAM bases throughout the world for other groups to pray over. Then he related several stories about how group prayers like this were specifically answered in the mission field.

"There was one time when our prayer threads led us to pray protection over a team in the middle of Africa," he said. "By connecting the common prayer threads, we saw that a mission team driving in a Jeep would be ambushed. A few months later, we learned that this actually happened, and miraculously they were saved from being harmed. We learned that this happened at the exact time when we were praying for them."

---

18   Intercessory prayer is the act of praying for what God wants you to pray instead of praying according to your own understanding.

This is what I'm craving, I thought. *Something alive and vibrant—a faith and relationship with God that's active and expecting great things!* I knew I needed to hear more, so I talked to one of the leaders after the meeting.

"I've been in and around church most of my life," I told him, "and I've never seen anything like this."

"Let me show you something," he said, handing me a paperback book titled *Go Manual* in bold letters on the front cover. It was a catalog of all the YWAM bases around the world and what each had to offer.

As I browsed through the book, a yearning deep within began to rise. I've always longed to travel—to see different countries and experience their cultures. Did God want me to be a missionary?

⁓

After that meeting, I couldn't get enough of YWAM and began making the journey to the mountain retreat center each week. I read through the *Go Manual* with an insatiable hunger. Suddenly, I knew what I was supposed to do—and my seemingly purposeless stagnation was sparked into action.

"What's next? How do I do this?" I asked an older leader at the mission base.

He smiled at my enthusiasm and told me to go through the manual and pick out four YWAM bases I was interested in. Then write to each one and wait to see which ones responded.

My top two choices were the bases in Switzerland and Guatemala, but Switzerland was my first choice. *Maybe that's just me,* I thought. I had had a Swiss foreign exchange student named Colin live with me for a school year, and his folks had invited me to visit someday. "Lord, You know," I prayed. "Please choose for me by making the right base the first acceptance I receive."

A month passed with no responses. Then one day, as I checked my mail at the post office, an envelope with the YWAM logo was on top of the pile. It was from Switzerland—my number-one choice. I had been accepted! I was so excited I felt giddy. I wanted to shout and couldn't wait to tell Mom, Brian, Kay, and Ida.

After receiving this confirmation, I knew God would help with the rest. I set my efforts on raising the money for my first six months in Switzerland. Since I was unemployed, this meant only one thing: I would have to sell everything I owned. Thanks to God's provision years before in bringing Ione Reget into my life, my only debts were my house and my car. Ione agreed to sell my house once I moved to Switzerland, and she bought my Ford Thunderbird for herself. She had always loved that car.

This left me with no transportation to drive to Mom's nursing home in Lone Pine, a fifty-five-mile journey each way. But Ida took care of that, happily driving me there three days a week. I'll never forget the day I told Mom about my desire to become a missionary. By this time, she was so weak she hadn't spoken a word in months. Even so, her mind was sharp, and her eyes filled with warmth.

She was sitting in the hospital bed when we came in that day, and she managed to give us a weak smile. I stood over her and held her hand.

"Mom," I said, "I have some good news." Her eyes looked right into mine as I spoke. "I believe God wants me to become a missionary. I've been accepted to a YWAM base in Switzerland."

A smile slowly spread across her face, and she tugged my hand, indicating that she wanted me to lean in.

"Go . . . for . . . it," she said in a hoarse whisper.

I pulled back and looked at her in amazement. If I needed more confirmation that I was making the right decision, this was it. I knew I would never leave as long as Mom was clinging to life, but I also knew she had given me her blessing.

～

Divesting myself of all my possessions—especially my dogs—was difficult. I was very close to my two cockapoos, and it broke my heart to say goodbye to them. They had been my constant companions over the past ten years. But I found them a really good home, which helped set my mind at ease. My material possessions were a little easier to part with, but selling everything didn't happen all at once. I had a lot of nice things because I had made good money with my television program and had nothing to spend it on except for myself. Although somewhat difficult, the process of divesting myself of my possessions was also incredibly freeing. Looking back, I see now how it was an outward expression of what was happening to me on a spiritual level. There I was, a new creation in Christ, letting go of every hindrance that could keep me glued to my previous life. God was helping me to walk a life of trusting Him.

How it would all work out, I had no idea. I only knew I needed to be obedient to what He had put in front of me, and He would show me the next step when I was ready. I took great comfort in this.

When it came to selling my furniture, Brian was my first customer; he bought my solid-oak four-poster queen-sized bed for his guest room. "Now when I visit you, I can sleep in my own bed," I told him.

Ida, Velma, and I also held a yard sale, which helped me sell my kitchen items, electronics, and other household goods. But for some reason, no one was interested in buying the most valuable items that remained: my solid-oak furniture.

It was around this time when I received a call from the nursing home that Mom was dying. She might not make it another day, they said. Ida and I immediately headed to Lone Pine. By the time we arrived, Mom was already gone. Although moved with remorse at not being with her when she passed, I was also consumed with an overwhelming sense of peace.

There hasn't been a day when I haven't missed her. No one could fill the void in my heart she had filled. And yet I knew where she was, and I knew I would see her again in heaven.

After the funeral, I purchased a one-way ticket to

Switzerland and prepared to leave the following month. Unfortunately, I still needed more money for expenses and was hoping to get it from selling my furniture. The week before I was scheduled to leave, I advertised in the local newspaper. However, the ad ran on a holiday weekend, and I had not received any calls. With just three days remaining before my trip, Ida, Velma, Ione Longest, and Dorothy were at my house playing board games when the phone rang.

"Are you still selling the furniture?" a lady asked. "Is it okay if we come by and take a look at it now?"

This was on a Sunday afternoon. An hour later, two women showed up and walked through each room. "We'll take it all," they announced, paying me the exact amount I was asking.

Ida, Velma, Ione, and Dorothy were watching the exchange and grinning. After the buyers left, they pointed up toward the ceiling, laughing. Did God have a sense of humor or what?

The buyers came back a few hours later with two men and loaded everything onto a moving van. It turns out the two couples were moving from LA to Lake Tahoe and had seen my ad as they were passing through town. As the van pulled away, we were hugging and laughing and crying. God had once again taken care of all my needs with perfect timing. When my mobile home was sold and I received half the proceeds from my mother's house, I would have all the money I needed to pay for a six-month term at the YWAM base in Switzerland.

My flight departed on June 13 from Los Angeles. As
I sat in my seat by the window, I watched the LA basin
grow smaller and smaller. Although my first semester in
Switzerland was only expected to be for six months, I had
an eerie feeling that I wasn't going to see LA for a very
long time.

Me with Mom a few weeks before her death, 1992.

26

THE LITTLE THINGS

As I stared out the small oval window of my plane above the Geneva airport, brilliant shades of green bedazzled my senses. A large lake stretched out at one end of the city, and I caught sight of a huge fountain shooting water high off the lake as we approached the landing. It was enchanting.

My friends the Bonnets were there to greet me when I walked into the terminal from the plane. It was so good to see someone I knew. Colin, the foreign exchange student I had hosted for one year while in Bishop, had a big smile on his face as he introduced me to his parents. I would be staying in their beautiful chalet in La Chau de Fonds for two weeks until the YWAM school started in Lausanne. This was my first introduction to Switzerland, and it couldn't have been any better. The Bonnets and I became very close, and they treated me like family. The time I stayed with them went by quickly, and they were soon driving me to the YWAM base in Lausanne.

I fell in love with Lausanne, Switzerland, from the

moment I arrived in July 1992. The cobblestone walkways and streets leading through cloisters of gray-stone buildings with red-tiled roofs and majestic cathedrals—it was all more wondrous than I had imagined. As I gazed over the expansive blue waters of Lake Geneva to the towering French Alps beyond, I couldn't believe I would be spending the next six months in such beautiful surroundings. I was excited with a sense of adventure, ready to go places and do things for God.

The YWAM base was located outside Lausanne, Switzerland (in Chalet-A-Gobet)—a historic three-story chateau gifted to YWAM as a school for training missionaries. The building sat against dark forest pines and bright green meadows. Students came from all over the world to be trained there, including a handful of Americans. Thankfully, most everyone spoke English. Now in my mid-forties, I felt comfortable with the other students. Most were single and in their thirties, forties, or fifties. There were also a few married couples.

⁓

The caliber of teaching and training provided by YWAM was high-quality, intense, and Bible-based. Speakers came from nearly every corner of the world, and students were constantly encouraged to learn the Bible and to be trained by it into evangelists, counselors, and teachers. Personal transformation was emphasized, and all students were expected to journal about what they learned and what God was speaking to them during their time in YWAM. Although I had never been much of a reader or writer, I embraced journaling while there. This discipline helped me to focus on my spiritual growth in ways I never could have imagined. Often, I didn't understand what was in my heart and what God was trying to speak to me until I started jotting things down. My journal entries were often inspired after truth-tablet taking, an exercise to help us consume God's encouragement.

"Imagine there are two tablets in my hand," my YWAM teacher said, holding out his hand as if holding two pills. "One tablet is precious, and the other is priceless. I am precious, and I am priceless in His sight." He mimed picking up one of the tablets and swallowing it. "I am precious in His sight," he said. Then he pretended to pick up the other tablet and swallow it. "I am priceless in His sight," he said. After this, he encouraged the class to do the exercise with him.

"You can take as many of these tablets as you want throughout the day, and they can only have a positive effect on you," he added.

It was a lovely way to remind us about God's love for us. Here is a journal entry I wrote after one of these exercises.

During our time of truth-tablet taking, the Lord impressed me to "take out from your Bible the prophecy your mother wrote about you." I thought it was only my thoughts, but after another nudge from the Lord, I finally took it out and realized that the Word from the Lord my mother had written in 1983 before I came back to Christ was intended for me at this precise moment!

At my mother's funeral, friends were getting up and

saying how my mom had encouraged them — some said that Mom had given them a word from the Lord, and they had it in their Bibles. I sat there wishing I had one of those words from the Lord in my Mom's handwriting.

About a month later, I was cleaning out my business file cabinet in preparation for Switzerland and YWAM, when I ran across this piece of paper hidden in a financial file. As I glanced over it, I became elated because I knew that it was a word my mother had written for me. Giving it only a cursory read, I decided to stick it in my Bible and take it with me to Europe so that I would always have it near to me.

As our little group prayed, I read it now with open eyes. The tears began to come as I realized that God knew ten years ago, and before I came back to the Lord in 1985, that I would be here in Lausanne in 1992, ready now to digest His direct Word for me.

I know He has specific work for me. "The in-depth thoughts and dreams of your life will surface into life-giving purpose." His purposes all along! Lord, let me carry out Your plan for my life in its fullness!

Next to this entry is the written prophecy from my mother glued into my journal:

Your life is indeed precious to Me, My son, and My plans for you will be fulfilled. Sin shall have no more dominion over you. Those sins which once held you fast have been broken, and with great joy, you shall draw water out of the wells of salvation.

I will strengthen, establish, and settle you as you

grow in Me. Look up and be at peace, for I am the mighty conqueror. The in-depth thoughts and dreams of your life will surface into life-giving purpose. You who have been forgiven much will love much—a love of which you have never known but shall know in its fullness. Each day of your life, I will make Myself more real to you, and you shall grow—yes, you shall grow.

God was indeed growing me daily while I was in YWAM training—changing my thoughts and attitudes. Often, He used simple circumstances to teach me. At other times, He used challenges and trials to reveal negative attitudes—symptoms of deeper issues that needed healing. As a loving Father, He started with the little things, and then He gradually worked His way to the more difficult strongholds in my life. It was all a process, and I needed to humble myself and allow Jesus to mold me.

I had been at the school for about three weeks when a group of students invited me to join them for a hike through the beautiful forestlands surrounding the campus. Although I had only brought two pairs of shoes to Switzerland—dress shoes and a new pair of white Reeboks—I gladly accepted. My new sneakers would have to do as footwear. But I forgot it had rained the night before.

At first, I tried to gingerly avoid the muddy puddles, but this soon proved to be an exercise in futility. The mud was everywhere, and my new shoes were covered with it by the time we arrived back at the school. I wiped them down and then headed to the laundry room and threw them into the nearest machine. Careful to keep the water cold, I set the temperature and waited. Unfortunately, I forgot I was dealing with Celsius instead of Fahrenheit, so what I thought was fifty degrees Fahrenheit was 122 degrees! Needless to say, my new shoes came out very clean but also one size smaller!

Inspired by the Lord's urging, I gave away my shrunk Reeboks to another student who had smaller feet and was in need. But now I was down to only one pair of shoes— my dress shoes.

Everything is expensive in Switzerland, and I had no money to buy a new pair of sneakers. The only thing I could do was to ask God to provide me with another pair.

After several weeks of tramping around the school in my dress shoes, the sneakers did come, but they weren't exactly what I had in mind. I found them while cleaning one of the vacated student rooms. All YWAM students were given work duties, and I was assigned maid services at this time. The sneakers were left under one of the beds. Elated, I examined them. The soles were still in good condition, but the canvas had several holes. One of the graduating students must have left them behind on purpose. I stepped out of my dress shoes and tried them on. They fit perfectly.

As I wore them around the school, I soon became known as "hole-y man." And while I enjoyed the affectionate teasing from my classmates, I wondered why the shoes had to be so ragged. *Lord, thank You for the shoes, but why couldn't You have given me newer ones?* I asked.

You didn't ask me for new shoes, the Lord responded.

Amazed, I started praying for new shoes—a bold request since I had no money. The next day, I walked downstairs to the dining room and checked my mail cubby. There was an envelope inside containing twenty-five francs! I had no idea who had given it to me, but YWAM leaders and students often blessed one another anonymously. I was grateful for the money, but I told God, "This isn't enough for shoes, but I'll trust You."

The twenty-five francs were still in my wallet a week later when I went with a small group of students on a picnic outing in the Alps. Our YWAM van broke down on the way back to base, so we started walking (this was before most people had cell phones). Just then, a nice couple pulled their RV over and asked if we needed a lift. The five of us enthusiastically crawled into the backseat of the large vehicle, and they took us to the outskirts of the nearest village. As we were walking to the train station, I noticed a shoe store with a rack of bargain shoes outside. *Maybe they have sneakers,* I thought as I headed over. There were several pairs on the rack, but only one was my size, and they fit perfectly. But could I afford them? I took them into the store and asked the price. The answer? Twenty-five francs! I was nearly dancing a victory jig down the street wearing my new shoes when one of my friends asked a question that caught me off guard.

"Why did you buy pink shoes?"

What? I looked down. To be more precise, they were gray and pink—I hadn't even noticed the pink. In frustration, I silently asked God, *Why did the shoes have to be pink?*

His answer came quickly. *You didn't say you wanted a specific color.*

I thought about this as we walked the next few blocks to the train station. God not only wants to bless His people in a general way but also specifically! What a loving Father He is. While this lesson about shoe color may seem trivial, it was part of my journey to wholeness and served to transform my prayer life and my trust in God's goodness throughout my life.

Because I had no spending money, I was never able to go out to dinner or on special trips that students had to pay for. One Saturday when most of the other students had gone home on break, a visitor came to tour the campus. Since I was the only person available and YWAM is known for its hospitality, I showed him around and explained the YWAM program to him. After the tour, we sat and had coffee in the dining room. He asked me where I was from and what I missed most about home.

"The flavor of Mexican food," I blurted out.

"Oh, well, you're in luck," he said. "I know of a Mexican restaurant in Lausanne. You should go there sometime."

I nodded and smiled, telling him I had heard of the restaurant and wanted to check it out. I didn't tell him I couldn't afford to eat out. The average dinner at restaurants in Lausanne amounted to thirty US dollars per plate—and this was in the 1990s!

The man must have sensed something because, as he was getting ready to leave, he pulled out his wallet and handed me forty francs! I tried to give him the money back, but he insisted. "No, you keep it," he said. "Go get yourself some Mexican food."

⁓

Communal living can feel like swimming in a fishbowl. Even in the best environments, strangers who become like family members can get on each others' nerves. In many respects, the base in Switzerland was no exception. What made things more challenging was many of us were from different cultures. Several of the students were from Great Britain, where they tend to be more reserved and polite. I, on the other hand, was demonstrative and extroverted. Add to that my background in the entertainment industry, and I must have appeared rather loud to these Brits. I knew this only because I was constantly reminded by them to lower my voice.

"Don't laugh so loud," they would say. "Keep your voice down."

Little did they realize that these "helpful" comments were doing serious damage to my psyche. I wasn't trying to be obnoxious; I was simply being me. Did I really need to change my personality to serve God?

I became a little depressed over this. *Can I do nothing right?* I prayed one night after a particularly cutting remark was made. *Why did You make me like this? If I'm supposed to be more reserved, then You need to help me change my personality.*

Not long after this, an Australian pastor who served in

Hawaii came to speak at the school. He was a large man with a bushy beard and jovial face; his deep voice resonated loudly when he spoke to the students.

"I'm an extrovert," he told us. "I come across as loud and boisterous. That's how God made me, and I use it for His glory. Others of you are introverts. You're quiet and reserved, and that's how God made you. Each of us needs to walk in the gifting and talents that God gave us. So if you're an extrovert, that's great. Praise God! Be an extrovert to the glory of God. And if you're an introvert, praise God. You were made to be that way. Don't let anyone tell you different."

At that moment, a few students in the class turned and looked at me. I winked at them, a big smile on my face. I was elated that God would speak directly to me like this in front of my fellow schoolmates. He had made me with this personality for a reason, and no one had the right to tell me otherwise. God had brought this man all the way from Hawaii to speak to me.

Since then, I've never struggled with feeling ashamed of my extroverted personality. God made me this way for His kingdom, and I'm thankful for it. In the same way, I've learned to value the personality traits of others—even those who are my opposite. Understanding this has allowed me to minister to people of all types because they know I value them for the way God created them to be. I've also learned to tone down my personality for the personalities of others.

These were some of the simple lessons God used to

guide me and teach me about Him. In His graciousness, He met me where I was at, but He didn't stop there. As I launched out into missions at YWAM, God started challenging me about much greater obstacles to my faith.

1992 graduating class,
YWAM Crossroads Discipleship Training School.

27

GROWING PAINS

After three months of training in Switzerland, it was time to serve as missionaries in other countries. I was part of a six-member team heading to southern Italy, Greece, and Israel.

Our first mission outreach was in the southern Italian city of Bari. We took prayer walks around the walled city and had discussions with curious strangers. Through our experiences of talking to people from different cultures and languages, we learned there are no barriers with Jesus. He breaks through it all.

One of my fondest memories was when our team led a beautiful Italian girl to the Lord. She was in her early twenties and was so kind and grateful for her new connection with Christ. She told her parents about her new friends, and they asked us over for dinner in their second home — an old-style, two-story country cottage nestled among an olive orchard. Its roof was flat, perfect for enjoying warm summer nights, and the pergola-covered patio housed a wood-fired pizza oven. The girl's family welcomed us with warm hospitality and showed us how to make our pizzas the Italian way. We sat into the evening, enjoying the delicious food and friendly faces of our hosts.

I had always longed for these kinds of cultural experiences and was amazed at God's goodness. It reminded me of what God had told me while I was praying during an overnight train ride from Milano to Bari.

It was the dead of night, and all my team members had bedded down in their sleeping compartments. But not me. I was wide awake and filled with excitement. I stood in the narrow wooden passageway as the train clacked across the dark Italian landscape. There were windows all along the passageway of this old sleeper car, and I pulled one down and leaned out, feeling the cool air rushing by my face and smelling the lush vegetation and dark soil.

This is where you belong, Wynn. This is what I created you for. A voice spoke in my thoughts. *Do you remember when you were a child and you used to sit in the backseat behind your dad as your family traveled on camping trips? I put a love for travel in you then, and now I'm calling it forth.*

Standing in that old train, just me and the Lord, I was overcome with emotion. God had a plan for me even as a child. And now the adventure had begun!

But adventures can come in all shapes and sizes.

After arriving in Sicily, I was contacted by the YWAM Crossroads Discipleship Training School (DTS) leader, Paul Marsh, who requested I fly back to Switzerland for a week to assist them in filming and producing a teaching series by well-known author and teacher Dean Sherman.

When the series was over, I flew back to southern Italy to meet back up with my team. It was early evening when my plane landed in Brindisi, a port city on the Adriatic Sea, and my team was waiting for me at the Italian port, where we would be catching a ferry heading for Greece. The ferry was set to leave in two hours. YWAM had supplied me with just enough money for a taxi ride there. Because I didn't speak a word of Italian, they also gave me a note with instructions to hand to a taxi driver.

When I walked outside the airport, I was confronted by a long line of taxi cabs. "Does anyone speak English?" I yelled.

One of the drivers rushed over, said something in broken English, and then picked up my suitcase and threw it into his trunk. I handed him my note. He scanned it and said, "I know where you need to go."

That's when I found myself being scurried along in a chaotic, white-knuckle ride through the streets of Brindisi. A lit cigarette hung from the driver's lips as he swerved in and out of traffic, all the while asking me a barrage of questions I couldn't understand. When he finally stopped at a deserted location in front of a locked gate, I had a feeling I had just been bamboozled.

"Are you sure this is where I need to be?" I asked.

"I am sure," he said in broken English.

I got out of the cab and stood near the gate. It was dark except for a distant streetlight near some buildings beyond the fence. Although the gate was secured by a chain and padlock, there was just enough room for me to squeeze through. But where was the ferry? Where were all the people and the shops? The place looked deserted. What was I supposed to do now?

The driver pulled my small suitcase from his trunk and pointed toward the light, indicating I needed to head that way. Then he got back into his cab.

"Are you absolutely certain?" I asked him again.

He nodded with confidence and drove off.

There didn't seem to be anything going on in the direction he had pointed, and I was trying hard not to let my fears overwhelm me.

I slipped through the gate, pulling my suitcase through after me, and started walking.

Mentally kicking myself, I headed toward the light and saw a small ticket shack with the lights on and people milling about. I poked my head inside. "Does anyone here speak English?" I asked.

A muscular young man in a tight green T-shirt came over. "I speak English," he said.

"Can you tell me where the Italian ferry is that goes to Greece?"

He walked outside and pointed to another section of the port across the bay, about three kilometers away. "That's where you need to go," he said. "Just follow those buildings over there, and it will take you to a taxi."

That can't be it, I thought. *I don't have any more money for a taxi, and I'll never be able to walk there in time.*

Even so, I had to try. I found a lighted section and began walking.

Then I heard someone call out my name. "Wynn, is that you?" Looking around, I saw one of my team members running toward me. "How did you know you were supposed to be here?" she asked.

"I didn't," I said. "I thought I was in the wrong place. I was just trying to figure out how I was going to get over there." I pointed across the bay.

My team member explained that they had been across the bay at first, but then they found out the Italian ferry workers were on strike. "We have to take a Greek ferry instead," she explained. "That's why we're here. To buy tickets for the other ferry. We were wondering how you were going to find us."

As the Greek ferry departed with me safely onboard, I thought about how the taxi driver just happened to know exactly where I needed to go. Did he know about the strike? Or was he an angel in disguise? Either way, I knew God had intervened.

⟿

I was looking forward to seeing the biblical sites in Greece and Israel. Little did I realize I was setting myself up for a big disappointment. We passed by many histor-ical locations in our van without stopping, and I had to constantly remind myself we were missionaries and not tourists. When we did stop at a few of the more popular sites, I was confronted with another problem: I couldn't afford the entrance fees. I only had one hundred francs in spending money, and I was determined to buy some "Jesus" sandals once we reached Israel. That meant that I had little left for anything else.

Three ladies in our group could easily afford to sight-see. They often took side excursions and enjoyed the cuisine at different restaurants, while the rest of us were left behind. The more this happened, the more resentful I became.

This resentment finally surfaced when we stopped at the Corinthian ruins and I couldn't afford the entrance fee. I was hoping I could at least see the ruins from a distance, but a fence blocked it from view. In desperation, I went over to the fence and tried to see the ruins through it, but a fiberglass shield was in the way. Overcome with frustration, I broke down into uncontrolled sobbing. That's right. I was having a full-on pity party. The two team members who were waiting at the van with me were also on a strict budget and could not afford to see the ruins. But they didn't seem resentful or upset. Instead, they were trying to comfort *me*. But I wasn't having any of it.

I was still sulking when the ladies returned to the van, and we headed to our next destination: Piraeus, a port city near Athens. Without realizing it, I began falling back into my old narcissistic patterns of behavior. I had completely forgotten to be grateful for all God had done for me and became focused instead on what I didn't have.

My bitterness blinded me from a simple fact: I had the money for the tour; I just chose to spend it on something else. Instead of taking responsibility for this choice, I found it more satisfying to blame God and feel sorry for myself.

Layer by layer, God was revealing deep patterns of resentment, and I began praying and thinking about my past. I had grown up in a loving home where there was only enough money to take care of our needs but never enough for extravagance. Was I resentful because of that? My mom used to say I had champagne taste on a beer budget. It wasn't until I worked as a sales rep for the beer distribution company that I started making real money. But instead of being wise with the money I earned, I squandered it on a hedonistic lifestyle.

I did buy those sandals in Israel, by the way. But they were cheaply made and quickly fell apart.

～

It seemed God wasn't wasting any opportunities to expose what lay under my good intentions and pious demeanor. Being the oldest member of my team, I often felt left out, like I was extra weight and wasn't needed. For example, everyone seemed to have a meaningful job except for me. Not that we all didn't have menial tasks to do. But I was the only person without an important job such as coordinating events, teaching, or leading worship as a musician or singer. The only job I was given was being the group's dishwasher. I couldn't understand why they didn't choose me as one of the singers, especially since they knew I had a background in professional singing and I thought had more talent and training than the woman they chose as the lead singer. This deeply offended me, and I felt unappreciated. My pride was wounded, and I fought daily against the ugly emotion of bitterness. Again, I struggled with taking offense. While my complaints remained unspoken, I cried out to God in frustration, *Is this all I'm here for? Just to wash dishes?* Like the patriarch Jacob, I wrestled with God, begging Him to use me—but on my terms, not His.

While I was struggling, Abba Father was standing with outstretched arms, wanting to free me from destructive patterns of thinking so He could bless me with greater riches than I had ever imagined—the riches of knowing Him more and being in His will and purpose. He seemed to be using this missionary trip not so much for me to minister to others but for Him to minister to me.

By bruising my pride, God was preparing me for a greater purpose. But I wouldn't realize what this was until I surrendered my pride and anger to Him.

Lord, I finally prayed one night, *it's for Your glory that I'm here, not mine. Please forgive me for my pride. Please heal my heart so I can serve You more completely in any capacity You want.*

After surrendering my pride, amazing things began to happen, but God still had more lessons for me. While in Israel, we attended a church service in Jerusalem. The church was a large Anglican cathedral within the walled city, and the liturgical service seemed dry and steeped in tradition. I immediately copped an attitude. *Why are we here?* I wondered. *This is ridiculous.* But God interrupted my thoughts when someone in the congregation stood up and gave a word in tongues—an unknown heavenly language. Then someone else stood up and gave the interpretation of the tongue.[19] I was amazed. This congregation seemed to be in the middle of a charismatic renewal!

Then I heard the Lord say to me, *Wynn, don't you ever think or say anything against my church again.* And I never have.

I wondered if it was the renewal that had attracted so many people to the service. All the pews were filled except for the row behind us, where three spaces remained empty. Were they being saved for someone? Just then, three young people made their way to the spot and sat down. They didn't appear to know anyone around them; it was as if God had saved the place for them. They looked to be about college age—two women and one man. The man was handsome, and I turned my gaze away to avoid the old temptation.

A soft voice came into my thoughts: *Him, Wynn.*

Thinking the voice could be from the enemy, I kept my gaze straight ahead, silently praying for strength.

The voice came again: *Him, Wynn.*

Confused, I asked silently, *Is this You, Lord?* For some reason, God seemed to be giving me a strong desire to connect with this young man, and it had nothing to do with physical attraction.

I want you to talk to him, came the voice.

When the service broke for parishioners to greet one another, I turned around to the group behind me and greeted each woman and then shook the young man's hand. We started talking, and there was an instant connec-

---

19   When God gives a message in a different tongue, He also provides an interpretation of what is spoken so that the congregation can benefit from it (I Corinthians 14:27–28).

tion. Although our conversation was brief, it was amazing how much information I discovered about him. His name was Chad, he was a college student from Chicago, and he was pursuing a career that would allow him to help legal immigrants adjust to the United States. He was in Jerusalem taking an eight-week course in Arabic.

The greeting time was soon over, and the service continued. But I felt the Lord still urging me to talk to Chad. Once the service ended, I looked for him, but he had disappeared into the crowd. The opportunity seemed to be lost. Our group wandered outside to the walled patio section, where the church was serving refreshments. I was standing with my team, munching on cookies and drinking coffee, when Chad walked over, and we continued our conversation. Outwardly, he seemed happy and confident, but I sensed something was troubling him. When I shared a little of my testimony, Chad was riveted.

"I've been praying God would send me someone I could talk to," he said. "And here you are!"

Chad began telling me some of his story. He had been repeatedly molested by men as a young boy. He wasn't homosexual as a result, but he was suffering from deep wounds and was too ashamed to seek help. Suddenly, all the pain I had been feeling about not being valued and having nothing to offer in God's service dissipated. It was like God was saying, "I brought you all this way for this young man." When my group started making movements to leave, I could tell that Chad wanted to talk more. But what could I do? I was with a group and had to go with them.

As we drove away, my frustration must have shown because our team leader asked me what was wrong.

I told her about Chad and the conversation we were having. "He's been through some really bad things, and I believe God has me here to talk to him, but I'm tied up with you guys."

She smiled and patted my hand. "We have all Thursday off. You can talk with him then."

"But I don't even know how to reach him."

"Why don't you try calling the office at the cathedral to see if he's still there?"

I didn't think there was any chance of that, but when we got back to our lodgings, I found the cathedral's office phone number and said a quick prayer. *Who knows?* I thought. *Maybe God will do something, and someone at the cathedral will know who he is and how to reach him.* I dialed the number. When the secretary answered, I described Chad to her and asked if anyone named Chad matching that description was still lingering around. To my amazement, she found him and got him on the phone.

Chad was glad to hear from me, and we arranged to meet at the cathedral on Thursday. When the day came, we spent hours sitting on the grass in a nearby park, sharing our stories. Chad had never found anyone he could talk to about his past, and I was able to minister God's Word to him and give him hope by sharing my testimony and the wisdom I had learned from God. When the van finally arrived to pick me up, we said goodbye, knowing a wonderful friendship had begun.

I visited him a few years later while on furlough in the

United States. He invited me to stay with him in Chicago before I flew home to California. When he collected me from the airport, he was glowing.

"I need to tell you something," he said, a shy smile playing on his face. "I met this girl, Christine. I think I love her."

We discussed some personal things from his past and how they might affect his relationship. Chad eventually married Christine and became a pastor. He and Christine have four children and remain happily married. Chad and I still stay connected through email and phone calls today.

God taught me so much from this mentor/friendship with Chad. I realized I had finally found my place in ministry—to help those who are relationally and sexually broken.

⸺

Little did I realize the wolf was waiting at my door, biding his time, waiting for the right opportunity to pounce.

In front of the Anglican church in the old city of Jerusalem.

Part of the YWAM team on the ferry to Greece. Among the seven are Dai Jenkins from Wales, Methat from Egypt, and Siew from Thailand.

In the passageway on the old train traveling through Italy.

Having in one of our rooms on the ferry from Greece to Israel.

*Making homemade pizzas in the countryside of Bari,
southern Italy.*

In the marketplace in Bethlehem, Israel.

In the Garden of Gethsemane, Israel.

Producing the two series of Dean Sherman,
Lausanne YWAM base.

Me and Chad.

28

THE FALL BACK

Standing at the sink in the men's restroom, I was trying not to think about what I had just done. But I couldn't help it. Over and over, it played through my mind like a taunting laugh. *You call yourself a Christian missionary? Get real. You'll never change. You're nothing but a phony—a filthy disgrace.*

I lathered my shaking hands and scrubbed them together, the cold water splattering from the faucet and turning the tips of my fingers blue. *How could I have fallen again? I had come so far.*

⤳

After our mission trip, I was invited to join a YWAM team in Holland for Mission 93, a conference with thousands of attendees from all over Europe. While there, I had another encounter that helped shape the way I minister to the sexually broken. I was eating lunch at a long table surrounded by young people when someone asked me to share my testimony. Afterward, a young Dutch man who was sitting at the other end of the table came over and introduced himself as Jeroen. He asked me how sexual abuse can affect relationships because his girlfriend, Mariska, had suffered as a child. Mariska joined us, and we continued to converse for over an hour discussing how God had walked me through a healing journey toward wholeness. This conversation began a healing journey for them, and we have kept in touch over the years. Jeroen and Mariska were eventually married and now have three children. It was a divine connection that I will always be grateful for.

As these kinds of interactions occurred, I learned to be more sensitive to my Father's leading. After returning to Lausanne, I started making plans for the future. Now that God had given me the heart to counsel and mentor others who were caught up in sexual addiction, I knew I needed some training in counseling. YWAM was offering a six-month counseling training school in Amsterdam, but I couldn't afford the six-thousand-dollar tuition fee. I prayed about it anyway. Shortly after, my brother sold my mother's mobile home for twelve thousand dollars and sent me half the proceeds. A few faithful supporters provided what I needed for travel. Everything was falling into place, and I was soon heading to Amsterdam.

It was amazing how God preserved me while there. Being the drug-and-sex-trade capital of the world, Amsterdam could have been my downfall. I must have had a host of angels stationed around me during this time, because I never felt tempted. I was consumed with learning everything YWAM could teach me about how to run a counseling ministry.

It wasn't until I returned to the base in Lausanne that I let my guard down, and the enemy was waiting.

I was out of money again, but the YWAM directors at Lausanne allowed me to live at the base as long as I worked there as part of the staff. There were eight of us on base tasked with keeping the gardens and lawns trimmed and working as the housing and kitchen staff. I was thankful God continued providing for my needs, but I was also starting to feel stagnant. When was He going to send me out for ministry?

Then things started shaking up at Lausanne. Loren and Darling Cunningham, YWAM founders, came to the base charged with making improvements where needed. What they found were a lot of incorrect attitudes among the leadership team and the students. Lausanne was the first base established by YWAM in 1970 and had become a monument unto itself. An attitude of complacency was evident, and objectionable habits that had developed over time had become more important than the vision of reaching the lost. Then the local fire department issued a citation regarding the disrepair of the building. It needed an overhaul to comply with code regulations. Drastic measures were necessary.

After several meetings, the YWAM leadership decided to close the base down for a season and send people elsewhere. Loren did this prayerfully, meeting with each staff member to find out what God had for them. My appointment with him was delayed due to a trip he had to take to Sweden. This delay only added to my sense of insecurity. After he returned a month later, I was certain he had forgotten about me. But then he called me into his office.

"You know," he told me, "I've been praying about you over the past month, and God gave me a Word. It's the scripture John 11:1: 'I go away to prepare a place for you.'" With a slight smile on his face and a glint in his eye, he said, "Wynn, I don't think He's calling you home to heaven just yet." He laughed. "I don't think He's going to take you back to the States either," he continued, "at least not permanently. I believe God has a place for you, but it isn't here, and it isn't in the United States. It's somewhere else. But you need to be patient."

Loren's words helped to calm my nerves, but I was still uneasy.

It was about this time when I was asked to help serve at a wedding in Einigen, the German part of Switzerland. The YWAM Einigen base was run by my friends Rudi and Eliane Lack in a summer home right above Lake Thun. Although I would be working at the wedding, any trip to Einigen was a welcome respite because Lake Thun was beautiful. The deep blue water surrounded by towering Alps and rich farmland would do me good.

Just before I left, I received some alarming news from home. One of my supporters wrote that she needed to stop supporting me because her son needed the money. That was half my financial support, which barely covered my basic needs.

The wedding went well, and Lake Thun was as delightful and serene as ever, but even the beautiful scenery couldn't nudge me into better spirits. My heart was in turmoil. As I rode on the train back to Lausanne after the wedding, I remember telling God, *You're not doing things fast enough. I'm about to run out of money and a position. Where am I supposed to go? What am I supposed to do?*

It wasn't that I was thinking about falling into sin and having sex with men again. I was just discouraged and feeling disillusioned. This made me a prime target for the enemy. When I felt close to God, I wouldn't even think about the old temptations that used to haunt me. But in an emotionally and spiritually weakened state, I was not thinking about being strong in the Lord. I was thinking about myself—that old childish, narcissistic attitude.

I got off the train and walked over to the bus station. While waiting for the bus to take me back to Lausanne, I went into the bathroom and stood at the urinal. Against my better judgment, I allowed thoughts of previous bathroom escapades to drift into my mind. That's when a very good-looking Swiss man came in and stood beside me. Within minutes, he propositioned me for sex, and I lost the will to say no. Seven years into my sobriety, I fell.

A shadow of doom and shame followed me back to Lausanne, and condemnation flooded me in despair. I tried to pray, but all that came out were excuses vented in anger toward God. *I don't have any money. I don't have anywhere to go. What did You expect would happen?* I went out to the grounds to mow the lawn and started sobbing—a real ugly cry from the deepest part of me. But the heaviness remained. For the next week, I wallowed in self-loathing, weeping uncontrollably whenever I was alone. For others, I tried to put on a false front as if everything were fine.

I was so consumed in shame and anger that I couldn't even repent for my sin. I expected God to do things my way, and when He didn't, I felt justified in my anger toward Him. God was trying to show me something much deeper than the sin I had committed, but I couldn't see it. It was all about personal autonomy. The reasons I had fallen and couldn't repent were because of my struggle to trust God at the deepest level—in my brokenness, self-pity, and self-loathing. It wasn't because I was harboring lustful thoughts about illicit sex. The old belief system that had caused me to fall away from God when I was a youth leader in my twenties was still hinged to my heart. As long as things were going well, I didn't have a problem with falling into temptation. But when things looked hopeless, it was right there to snag me and pull me under. Instead of fighting against the temptation, I used excuses to turn back to my sin.

Like many, I was under the impression that I was immune from temptation because I was saved and faithful in following God's Word. But the Bible doesn't say that. Rather, it says we will be tempted, and we better be prepared:

No one undergoing a trial should say, "I am being tempted by God," since God is not tempted by evil, and he himself doesn't tempt anyone. But each person is tempted when he is drawn away and enticed by his own evil desire. Then after desire has conceived, it gives birth to sin, and when sin is fully grown, it gives birth to death (James 1:13–15 CSB).

Anyone can be tempted; temptation is not sin. It's when we are drawn away by our evil desires that the temptation turns to sin as we act it out. My evil desires were self-pity and self-preservation. I became more concerned over my sanity and personhood, ignoring that my value comes from God. Pure and simple, I was in rebellion. I should have stopped and analyzed my thoughts, focusing on Jesus's words:

> A thief comes only to steal and kill and destroy. I have come so that they may have life and have it in abundance (John 10:10 CSB).

God had already provided a way of escape through His Word, but I was too focused on me to realize I could trust Him even when the circumstances indicated otherwise.

When a female friend asked me and my roommate, Kent, over for dinner, I accepted, figuring the distraction might do me good, and I loved the idea of a home-cooked meal. After we ate, we sat around the small kitchen table talking, and a picture of the words "James 5:16" floated into my mind. I couldn't remember what James 5:16 said, so I asked if I could see her Bible. She handed me an amplified version, and I looked up the scripture, reading it silently to myself:

> Confess to one another therefore your faults (your slips, your false steps, your offenses, your sins) and pray [also] for one another, that you may be healed and restored [to a

spiritual tone of mind and heart]. The earnest (heartfelt, continued) prayer of a righteous man makes tremendous power available [dynamic in its working].

I knew the Lord was speaking to me. I looked at Kent, one of the kindest young men I have ever known. He would be a good person to confess to. But our female friend wasn't so guarded with people's stories, so I didn't feel safe making a confession with her in the room. I told them only that I had fallen into sin and that I needed to confess it—no other details. They listened and then prayed for me, but the heaviness was still with me when Kent and I returned to our dorm room at the YWAM base.

Kent must have sensed it, because he said, "I'm willing to stay up a little longer if you want to talk."

My words came out slowly at first, cautiously. But then they began to flow like a river. I told him everything—not just about my recent fall but about my struggles with sexual addiction throughout my life. It was the first time since I had left the United States that I had said anything about it.

While I talked, I watched Kent's face for his reaction. He looked concerned but not shocked or disgusted. When I finally finished, he came over and put his hands on my shoulders. Then he said a very simple, sweet prayer. At that moment, something changed in me. I can't describe what shifted, but the heaviness was suddenly lifted and was replaced by a deep sense of joy.

This experience taught me about the importance of having a safe place to pour out our souls. If it hadn't been

for Kent's willingness to be obedient to God in this way, I
would have missed this opportunity for healing and transformation.

"There's something different about you," a pastor told
me the following day after church service.

I smiled, still feeling remnants of joy from the previous
evening. Then I glanced at Kent and said, "God's doing
some things in me."

"Yes," the pastor said. "I can tell. You look much
brighter."

The YWAM base under construction in Lausanne, 1995. Loren and Darling Cunningham are standing in the forefront.

My roommate, Kent; another friend; and me standing near the Matterhorn on a day outing from the YWAM base in Lausanne, 1993.

29

WOMEN IN AUTHORITY

Ever since I had been molested by a woman when I was eleven, then forcibly dealt with by our senior pastor (another woman) and shamed by a woman police detective when I was thirteen, I had had a problem with women authority figures. It wasn't until years later that I realized the exact time when this resentment turned into rebellion. It was when my mother had arranged for me to be prayed over by the group of women from our church. Their intention to cast a demon of homosexuality out of me had backfired, and a spirit of fear had invaded my mind: fear of women. Since then, I had found myself in silent rebellion and mistrust whenever a woman was placed over me in a position of authority.

When I surrendered my life to Christ and became a dedicated Christian, my problem with women authority figures didn't end. Instead of dealing with my hostility toward them, I avoided the issue, thinking it would go away. When I arrived in Switzerland and found that a husband-wife team was in charge of the YWAM Discipleship Training School, I was relieved. At least there would also be a man in leadership.

This didn't last long, however, because in almost every YWAM training and mission I was involved with, I had at least one woman leader over me. While I got along with most of them, there were a few very dominant and controlling personalities who stirred up that old rebellion. I felt threatened and often went into a private mental battle, trying to stuff my emotions and deflect my feelings whenever I was around them.

God finally forced me to face the issue after the Lausanne base was closed, and I was invited by the Lacks to work as part of the housing staff at Einigen. Although Rudi and Eliane Lack were great friends who mentored me during my time there, Rudi was often called away on mission trips, and Eliane was left in charge. There was also a young Swiss-German woman with a strong personality who ran the kitchen. Like the other staff members at the base, I had many duties in and around the property. It took at least eight people to make the hospitality facility run efficiently. Being a fast worker, I would get my chores done quickly so I could have extra free time to study. Many of my ministry's foundational ideas came to me during this time.

However, my American sense of efficiency was not understood by the European staff members. They tended to work more methodically, making sure they completed whatever task was required in the time allotted. They

couldn't understand why I would hurry through my
chores. The young lady who directed the kitchen was
especially antagonistic. Even though my results were
the same as those of the other staff members, she became
upset whenever she found me studying in my room
during chore time. "I finished all my work," I would tell
her. But this didn't matter. She seemed convinced I was a
lazy American slacking off while other people were still
working, and she often browbeat me.

When I had had enough of her treatment, I scheduled
a meeting with her and Eliane. They were sitting rigidly
in their chairs when I walked in the room. I listened while
the young woman voiced her complaints about me. Eliane
nodded her head in agreement with the young lady's
accusations, and I became more and more annoyed as my
explanations seemed to be falling on deaf ears.

"What do you want me to do?" I finally asked. "Do
you want me to fill up the extra time with more work?"

They looked confused and said that I was making
excuses. Why couldn't they understand that thorough
efficiency—quickly done or not—was a good thing and
not something to be frowned on? Our conversation was
going nowhere, and I was pretty upset. When I went back
to my room, I expressed my frustration in prayer. *This
doesn't make any sense. Why should I have to work in this way
just to please them when they're the ones being unreasonable?*

After a while, I heard the Lord say, *Trust Me, Wynn.
Humble yourself for My sake.*

At first, I resisted this instruction. Why should I do
that? I didn't do anything wrong! But when I finally

surrendered my will to God's will, a sense of peace filled me. *Lord, what do You want me to do?*

After several minutes of silent meditation, I had my answer.

The next day, I quickly went through all my chores as usual. But instead of going back to my room, I went to the kitchen leader and said, "I'm done with my regular chores. What would you like me to do now?"

She was speechless. After thinking for a minute, she said, "All is covered. Do what you want to do until dinner. I'll need you again then."

And that was it. From then on, both she and Eliane began to acknowledge my hard work, and life around the base became joyful. God was showing me that I needed to rest in Him during these times of struggle and ask Him for wisdom and discernment. I realized I can waste so much time worrying about my struggles and getting caught up in an emotional upheaval because I'm too focused on myself. It might be that the struggle isn't even about me. Instead, God might be trying to reach someone else. Even so, He can still grow me closer to Him through it. It's amazing how peacefully we can resolve conflict when we confront issues with love, truth, and humility. I'm happy to say Eliane and I have a friendship that has stood the test of time—a friendship I have always cherished.

Not long after this, my friend Bartho, a YWAM graduate, sent a fax to me from South Africa, his home country. He had an interesting question: "Many young people in our area are suffering from sexual abuse and brokenness. They could use your help. Would you like to join us as a leader in our youth ministry?"

Although this was the kind of direction I was seeking, the idea of flying to South Africa seemed impossible. Where would the money come from?

"Ha," I wrote back. "Like I'm just going to fly down there with no money."

"God will provide" was his only reply.

I told Rudi and Eliane about his invitation, along with a mature Christian couple named Dai and Shirley who lived in England. They agreed to pray with me about it. I also wrote to Ida in Bishop, and she started a prayer chain. Although strangers to each other, they all came to the same conclusion. After three weeks of praying, they agreed this was God's direction for me. I also felt peace from God. But where would I get the money?

On the lawn in front of the YWAM base,
Einigen, Switzerland, 1994.

Singing with Anna on the piano in the Schlössli "Le Rüdli"
YWAM base, Einigen, Switzerland, 1995.

Left to right: Rudi Lack, kitchen worker, Anna, me, a French missionary, Eliane Lack, and a volunteer worker having breakfast one morning, 1995.

In my room at the YWAM base in Einigen, Switzerland, 1995, working and writing my teachings.

Eliane Lack, kitchen worker, and me in the kitchen working in the YWAM base in Einigen, Switzerland, 1995.

Dai and Shirley Jenkins on a day trip in England in 1998.

*A view of the Schlössli "Le Rüdli" YWAM base,
Einigen, Switzerland, 1995.*

30

PREPARING FOR
SOUTH AFRICA

If I was ever going to make it to South Africa, I would need money to not only get me there but also to support me while there. I couldn't raise the money in Switzerland because I didn't have a church network to draw supporters from or a work visa. My only choice was to return to the United States and find a job.

Bishop was still my hometown, and that's where my brother and his family lived, so that's where I returned to look for work. I stayed with my brother and his wife and applied for every job I could, but nothing panned out—not even for a minimum-wage position. After several weeks with no luck, I was becoming discouraged.

Maybe God wasn't calling me to be a missionary after all, I thought. Or maybe He had another plan for me. These notions seemed to fight against my very being. Could I still praise Him, knowing I may never be what I had come to believe He created me to be? God had put this wanderlust in my heart and had given me all this international training. Was I supposed to just stay at home? I knew I had to settle this in my mind.

Finally, I came to the end of myself and surrendered the battle in my thoughts to God. I gave up trying to make it happen.

"Okay, Lord," I told Him. "If You want me to stay here, I will. This isn't about me. It's about You, and I trust You."

The very next day, a Realtor friend called me with an opportunity. He had taken a side job as a location manager for a film production company that was planning to shoot some footage for the movie *The Arrival*, a science fiction thriller written and directed by David Twohy. The movie starred Charlie Sheen and costarred Ron Silver, Teri Polo, and Richard Schiff. It was primarily being filmed in Mexico, but the production company was drawn to the Big Pine area near Bishop because the script called for the use of the astronomical radio telescope array located at Owens Valley Radio Observatory. My friend told me the production company needed a production assistant for the next three weeks, and he thought I would be a perfect fit due to my background in the entertainment industry.

A "production assistant" is a fancy title used for a gofer, an errand boy for the director and the production manager. I would make $850 working this job, and although I needed to raise $1,300, it was a good start. Then, halfway through the job, the production manager asked me to take Polaroid photos of people who were interested in jobs as extras—people who would appear in the film but have no dialog lines. The photos were then shipped by FedEx to the director in Mexico so he could decide who to use for the film once they started shooting in California. During this time, the director said he also needed four stand-ins for the main stars. While I was taking photos of people who were applying for these positions, a team member suggested he take my picture and have me apply for Charlie Sheen's stand-in position.

"You're about his height and weight," he told me. "Why don't you include your picture?"

The position would give me an additional one hundred dollars per day, so I thought, *Why not?* To my amazement, they hired me! This boost gave me all but one hundred of the money I needed. Then a friend donated the additional one hundred, and I had it.

It wasn't until I was on the plane leaving the United States that Loren Cunningham's word from the Lord came back to me: "I go before you to prepare a place." It occurred to me that God had been working behind the scenes the entire time. He knew exactly when the time was right for me to leave and had orchestrated it that way. God was still teaching me to trust Him, something I struggled with due to the many hurts and wounds of my past.

The moment my plane landed in Cape Town, South Africa, I felt at home. A welcome and friendly face greeted me at the airport—Bartho, the young man with whom I had worked on the YWAM base in Lausanne. From Cape Town, we journeyed to Strand, a seaside resort community about fifty kilometers away and situated on the northeastern edge of False Bay in the foothills of the Hottentots Holland Mountains. Strand's blue waters and long beaches along the South Atlantic Ocean contrasted beautifully with the lush grasslands and sloping mountains that rose from the sea. It was very different from the lush greens and rocky cliffs of Switzerland yet still dazzling. I couldn't believe this was where I would be living.

Ebed, the church where Bartho worked as a youth pastor in Strand, was primarily a white Afrikaans congregation. While most spoke English, their native tongue was Afrikaans. They were a very warm and friendly group, and Bartho made it his duty to introduce me to everyone. He was engaged to be married but still living in a bachelor flat, as they call apartments in South Africa. He set me up to live with him there until I could find another place of my own. The flat was spartan with a twin bed and a child's armoire, where I could store only two or three items of clothing. The kitchen was basic: one cabinet, no counter space, and two hot plates sitting atop a small oven supported by a short-legged galvanized table. One of my donors who lived in Switzerland graciously sent me enough money to cover my rent each month, so everything seemed to be falling into place.

Although I had little experience teaching youth about sexual brokenness, I was fairly confident I could handle it. I studiously organized and assembled all the notes and teachings I had accumulated while serving in YWAM, ready to fill the youth with God's wisdom.

I had no idea how unimpressed they would be.

The youths met every Wednesday night in a room on

the church campus. They were sitting in a circle when I entered with my three-ring binder filled with notes and outlines. Bartho introduced me and then led the small group into a few worship songs. When I started to teach, I was unprepared for the twenty unresponsive, bored faces staring back at me. Undaunted, I launched into my lesson with as much false exuberance as I could muster. What I lacked in self-confidence, I made up for in handouts. When the meeting was over, I encouraged them to read the material so we could discuss it at the next meeting. I was trying not to be discouraged by their lackluster attitudes but was only kidding myself. I was no longer that hip young man who played guitar when I led a youth group so many years before. Now almost fifty, I hadn't picked up a guitar in over twenty years. I wasn't used to teenagers and had lost touch with how to reach them.

Bartho tried to be supportive, giving me helpful tips on how to work with young people. "This isn't a group of young adults who are here because they choose to be," he explained. "Most of these kids are here because their parents bring them. We have to meet them where they are."

I told Bartho I understood, but I didn't change my methods. After three weeks of trying to force-feed them information, Bartho sat me down. "This isn't going to work," he said. "Perhaps you are not meant to teach youth."

I knew he was right, and I felt defeated and devastated. *God, why did You bring me over here if I can't do this?*

During a five-day backpacking trip on the Otter Trail in South Africa, 1997.

Doing one of my favorite things:
petting cheetahs on one of the reserves in South Africa.

Out for a meal in the Cape with Bartho, Landi, and a friend.

31

FINDING MY FEET

When my tourist visa expired, I was away in Switzerland collecting the rest of my belongings and reapplying for another tourist visa for South Africa. During this time, Bartho married the woman he was engaged to. He was living with his wife when I returned, and I took over his apartment.

Somehow, I knew God wasn't finished with me in South Africa, so I tried to be faithful to Him by attending all the church events and by serving wherever I was asked. To my delight, God began to move.

I made many good friends at Ebed and was often invited to families' homes for meals and gatherings. Soon, people began stopping by my flat to talk and share a hot cup of coffee. Many visits turned into one- or two-hour counseling sessions. It wasn't unusual for me to have two or three unexpected visitors in one day. After hearing of this, my nephew's wife, Sherri, created a sign for my mantel that read "WYNN'S COFFEE SHOP—CUPS OF WISDOM

SERVED UP HERE." While this was meant for fun, it was also true that people valued the conversation and enjoyed the coffee. I never advertised, and I can't explain why I received so many visitors. My church family seemed to recognize I had been blessed with the gift of counseling.

The pastor of Ebed asked me to share my testimony with the congregation one Sunday night. Ironically, God used me to reach the youth through that service but not in the formal way I had envisioned. It started when a couple of high-school seniors approached me after I shared.

"We have a group of guys that meet in my home on Friday nights," the taller of the two stated. "We're just some friends who get together once a week to worship and discuss spiritual matters. Would you like to join us?"

Their invitation surprised me. Why would a group of senior high-school boys want me to join their group? But I sensed God was influencing their request, and I agreed to join them.

As I entered the young man's house, the five teenagers lounging around on couches and chairs warmly greeted me. They spent the first ten minutes joking and telling stories. One of them picked up a guitar and started playing worship music. Then they all began singing. When the worship ended, they talked about their struggles in school, their coming graduation, and the challenges they had in following their faith. I listened, absorbed in their stories. It was amazing how quickly they accepted me into their group. They were eager to ask for my thoughts on some of the issues they were facing, and over time, we became good friends. In one sense, I was their unofficial mentor and was able to help them navigate through some difficult times in their lives. I learned to listen more and talk less.

How different this was from my first experience with the Ebed youth! I continued to attend their weekly gatherings for as long as they lasted, and I still keep in touch with most of them. Some are even part of the inner core of my ministry family. Although now successful men with families of their own, they have helped support me through encouragement, prayer, and finances.

With the friendships I was making came connections and then invitations to speak. I was soon being invited by various churches throughout the region as a guest speaker. This was all happening without any self-promotion. It was only by word of mouth. God was showing me that if I was faithful in what He was putting in front of me, He would take care of the rest.

Almost immediately, I noticed a great need in South Africa for a ministry to help the sexually broken. The sex trade in pornography and prostitution was rampant, as were sexual molestations, homosexuality, adultery, and rape. Nearly everywhere I went, people approached me with heartbreaking stories. No wonder God had brought me to South Africa.

In addition to speaking in churches, I was also invited to speak to students, teachers, and administrators at public high schools. The experience brought back memories of touring Central America as a young man. God had used those experiences to teach me how to relax in front of different audiences. Instead of being nervous, I enjoyed these engagements.

It was during this time that a small group of friends from Ebed suggested we hold a men's conference on sexual brokenness. Through their connections, we were able to book three well-known speakers, including a famous football (soccer) star named Schalk Burger Snr and Regardt van den Bergh, a South African film and teleision actor, film director, and screenwriter—both strong Christian leaders in their vocations. Our conference, Men of Commitment, also featured a popular Pentecostal pastor named J. E. Samuel.[20] Nearly 250 men filled the auditorium for two days of anointed teaching.

The conference was so well received that invitations for speaking engagements began pouring in from throughout the region.

"You need to work with the churches in this area because we need a ministry like this, and we have no one," Pastor Samuel told me afterwards.

But how would I do that? I had heard about a group named TRAILBlazers that was already working through several churches in South Africa to bring wholeness and healing to the sexually broken, but I had never been able to connect with them. Their ministry was mostly in the northern region and not where I was located in the south. Then one day I received a call from Roger and Josephine, the leaders of TRAILBlazers. They were organizing a

---

20   This name has been changed to protect the pastor's privacy.

two-day seminar at one of the churches in Cape Town and needed another speaker.

After praying about the invitation, a sense of peace filled me. God was providing connections, and I realized this was yet another step along the way. I agreed to teach at the seminar, which went very well. The TRAILBlazers curriculum dovetailed right into my ministry. Roger and Josephine noticed this as well and asked me afterward if I would be interested in adopting the TRAILBlazers name for my ministry in the Cape area.

I prayed about it and talked it over with some leaders I was raising up from my support group. Everyone agreed this was a blessing from God, and we named the ministry TRAILBlazers-CAPE.

Our first Men of Commitment seminar in Strand,
South Africa, 1996.

The high-school seniors who took me into their group, 1996
(top to bottom: Werner, Andreas, MP, Gerhardt, and Bernie).

Our first ministry support group in Strand,
South Africa, 1998.

My prayer wall at my flat in Strand, South Africa.

32

CHALLENGES OF GROWTH

Opportunities to speak and conduct seminars became available throughout the Cape region, and I quickly realized
this was becoming bigger than one man could handle. I
assembled a group of about twenty-five people who had
experienced sexual brokenness in their lives. We became
a large support group, meeting weekly to review and
discuss our spiritual growth. Many of these individuals
became the foundational team for the emerging ministry
that God was creating.

I also started putting more energy into training leaders
to help in the ministry. This proved to be difficult, however.
Because addicts and broken individuals are on a journey
of healing and wholeness, they must first become more
stable in their walk with the Lord and their commitments
before they are ready for leadership. This process can take
years.

During this time of pressure from the growing ministry, I was invited to give my testimony at Atlantic Christian
Assembly in Sea Point. Afterward, Anthony, the Sea Point

senior pastor, called me with a proposal. He wanted me to run the TRAILBlazers-CAPE ministry from his church in Sea Point and would provide me with free office space if I agreed to do so.

"Our church shares a neighborhood with prostitutes, drug addicts, and gay bars," he explained. "We need someone here who can effectively minister to these people."

The office had four rooms, a kitchen, and a bathroom. I would be sharing it with a woman named Marge Ballin, a former YWAM missionary who was operating a ministry for sexually broken women.

I was still living in Bartho's old apartment at the time but now had a car that someone had given me and could make the forty-five-minute commute each day. Still, this would be an additional strain on my already limited budget. How would I pay for the fuel and the wear and tear on my old car? Silently, I took the matter to God. "Lord, I see the need, and I see the opportunity, but is this really from You? How can I possibly take on this added expense?"

I also took the matter to my seven-member board of directors and asked them to pray for guidance. After a few days, we met again, and the answer was unanimous. They all felt this was a door God was opening. I meditated on scripture, especially Proverbs 11:14: "Where there is no guidance, a people falls; but in the abundance of counselors there is safety." The presence of God's peace filled me.

"Okay, Lord," I told God. "You've provided for all my needs so far, and I'm going to trust You here as well."

And He did provide. As soon as I started making the commute to Sea Point, the extra funds I needed began coming in—even from new people who had never given to the ministry before. Most of them had heard my story, and it gave them hope. "What the world needs now is love . . ." That song floated through my head, and I realized that the world needed more than love. It needed hope. Because of what God had brought me out of and what He had been doing in my life, people saw and felt hope and were encouraged. I never asked for money except for the classes we held, yet there was such a hunger for something good, something better. We were offering hope, and people were responding.

Opportunities for ministry and speaking engagements were flooding in so rapidly that I could barely keep up with the requests. I focused on raising up specific leaders to help me meet the demands of preparing, organizing, and teaching throughout the region.

One of the biggest challenges we found was the lack of teaching materials on the subject for pastors. This was a crucial need because most pastors had no experience dealing with sexual addiction. To help address the need, my team—Dale and Gillian Marsberg, Margaret Logan, Yvonne O'Connor, Sue Klopper, and others—helped me cobble together a leadership training manual. They supported me as part of the board, teaching staff, and wise counsel. In short, they became my family. Together, we spent over a year training the leadership team. Our mission was to help churches set up counseling and support groups for individuals seeking help. By using our material, churches would then be able to help people understand how Jesus can bring healing and wholeness to specific broken areas of their lives. We started with a very simple premise: For the broken to get the help they need, they must discover where they are broken.

We were booked solid for the next four years, training church leaders on how to understand and help their congregants. We named the manual *TRAILBlazers-CAPE Restoring Wholeness Leadership Course.*

~

As things came together and the ministry was called on to participate in more speaking engagements and conferences, I began looking outward for similar ministries that we could partner with. At the top of my list was an organization called Living Waters, founded by Andrew Comiskey. This was an intensive thirty-week program based in America, which I had heard about while at YWAM Amsterdam. The program was extremely in-depth, focusing on freeing people from sexual abuse, addiction, and bondage. I had always wanted to participate in it as a student, but God never opened that door while I lived in Europe. In 2001, I contacted Andy to see if he would be interested in bringing his group to the Cape to conduct a seminar with TRAILBlazers-CAPE. When I think about this now, I laugh because we lacked the resources to conduct a seminar of this magnitude; but God had increased my faith, and I trusted Him with the logistics. The Lord did not disappoint. A member of my team had a friend who graciously donated his beautiful bed-and-breakfast in Green Point for Andy's team. Others provided all the food we needed during the four-day event.

The seminar was a complete success, with hundreds of attendees being trained and all receiving deep ministry from the Holy Spirit. Afterward, Andy invited me to participate in the Living Waters training in Johannesburg, and I eagerly accepted. Andy has been a great encouragement and example to me. This training solidified my understanding of sexual sin and all the entanglements that come with it—how it not only affects the lives of those directly involved but also how the families and friends have both contributed to and are affected by it. The training provided more insight into my journey and helped me better understand my past, giving me the tools I needed to minister with more effectiveness.

After the training, Andy asked if I'd be interested in becoming the Living Waters coordinator in the Cape, but I didn't accept. I knew God wanted me to focus on the ministry He had already started in TRAILBlazers-CAPE. Even so, I volunteered to help them coordinate events in the area when needed, and I have remained active in the Living Waters circle of influence. I've also led a few Living Waters support programs while in South Africa. Studying and working with Living Waters has helped me to understand more clearly the difference between our two ministries. While TRAILBlazers-CAPE focused on guiding the broken into the waters of recovery, Living Waters helped them dive deeper. There is a great need for both forms of ministry, and they complement each other.

⤳

Throughout this time, the Cape turned out to be the perfect location for our ministry because it was centrally located and not too far from most of the places we were asked to minister. We now had our separate board of directors, nonprofit status, a PO box, phone numbers, and a bank account. The ministry was beginning to grow exponentially with support groups running all the time.

At the height of this growth, the main TRAILBlazers organization was struggling. They were located in Johannesburg and were having trouble expanding their ministry. I received a call from Roger at the main office one day, who announced they had decided to move the main organization to the Cape and work with Pastor Samuel in Stellenbosch. As I sat with the phone receiver cradled between my neck and shoulder, I wasn't sure how to respond. Finally, I said, "Okay, how's that going to work?"

"You'll need to give up the TRAILBlazers-CAPE name," Roger said.

At first, I was speechless. Then I said, "Okay, I'll let my board know."

My knee-jerk reaction toward anger and self-pity tried to rear its ugly head, but I knew better than to listen to those voices. Instead, I silently prayed. "Lord, You know what You're doing. Help me to understand and guide me."

Then I called an emergency board meeting and told them the news.

"Good," one of the members said. "This is God." The

other members agreed. Things had been a bit strained between TRAILBlazers-CAPE and the main office for some time. We knew this was God's way of telling us it was time to amicably separate and begin to run the ministry the Lord was leading us to do.

We got to work immediately. Our first task was to create a new name for the ministry. At first, we were at a loss, but then I saw it. Our manual was sitting on the table in front of me titled *TRAILBlazers-CAPE Ministries Restoring Wholeness Leadership Training Course.* We were already using the term "Restoring Wholeness" as part of our name, and it was a perfect description of what we were trying to achieve. Within a few weeks, TRAILBlazers-CAPE officially became Restoring Wholeness Ministries. The Lord walked with us through the transition, and it went as smooth as butter.

Our first Living Waters group in the Cape.

*The front of our office in Atlantic Christian Assembly
(Now LIFE Church, Sea Point), 2000.*

Our first leaders of TRAILBlazers-Cape, 1998.

Our first ministry board in South Africa.

*Visiting past Restoring Wholeness leaders
during my last trip to South Africa.*

Waiting for a train in Slovakia, 1999.

33

A SON

A snare that successful ministry leaders can easily fall into is to get ahead of what God is doing and start assuming that every invitation comes from God and should be immediately accepted. I made this mistake when my friend invited me to join an organization called Exodus Europe, Middle East, and Africa. The organization was based in Europe and acted as an umbrella ministry for other ministries that served people in relational and sexual brokenness. Board members spoke and trained in conferences throughout Europe, Africa, and the Middle East. I was thrilled to be invited and believed it was God's will. But God's will does not always mean God's timing. Being part of Exodus required me to attend board meetings twice a year. These meetings were held mostly in Europe, and I did not have the money for the plane tickets. So I started using my credit card for the trips, and the debt began piling up. At the time I'm writing, I've just finished paying off that credit card bill. The lesson? There are consequences to not waiting on God—even when you are trying to do things in His name.

Today, I never go anywhere unless the money is available in advance for my travel expenses.

Still, God did some tremendous things through my alliance with Exodus in Europe, especially when I was invited to speak at a two-day seminar in Israel. This seminar was at the very same Anglican church where I met Chad. As I stood in this austere church as a keynote speaker in front of a large congregation, the magnitude of it overwhelmed me. My voice quivered as I spoke into the microphone. "This is where God first called me to help the sexually broken," I told the audience. "In His mercy, He has seen me through it all and has managed to use me in such a powerful way for His glory."

When I returned home to Cape Town after this trip, a young man called me for an appointment. His name was Edmund, and he said he learned about me through a magazine article he ran across at a doctor's office. Oddly enough, the article had been published two years earlier and described how I had left the homosexual lifestyle and was now helping the relationally and sexually broken in South Africa.

If this man can change, maybe I can too, Edmund thought.

We made plans to meet a few weeks later at my office in Cape Town, but Edmund never showed up. Worse still, he didn't call to cancel the appointment.

"Well, I guess that's that," I said to myself. "Too bad."

Call him, the Lord whispered.

"Lord, You know my rule. I don't chase after people who don't show up for their appointments."

Call him.

Apparently, God didn't think much of my rules. I knew better than to argue, so I called.

Edmund apologized profusely for missing the appointment, and we set another date for the following day. Then he missed that appointment too.

"I told You this would happen," I said out loud to God. But He wasn't having any of it.

Call him again.

"Really?"

Feeling like a mother hen, I called Edmund for the second time.

"Hi, Edmund, this is Wynn Thompson. We had an appointment—"

"Oh, no!" came the voice on the receiving end. "I'm so sorry. Can we reschedule?"

"That's why I'm calling." I was trying hard not to have an edge in my voice.

"Can I come tomorrow at one?" he asked. "I promise I'll be there this time."

But when 1 p.m. came and went, there was still no Edmund. I rose from my chair and walked from my office through the hallway that led to the front door. When I looked toward the locked iron gate protecting the church property, I saw a young man pacing back and forth on the sidewalk.

"Edmund?" I called out. "Is that you?"

"Yes, it is," he said.

I pressed the button to open the gate. "Come in, please. I'm Wynn."

Edmund was a tall, light-skinned Black man in his early twenties, with large brown eyes and a captivating smile. But Edmund didn't smile much when I first met him. He was nervous and jittery, and he spoke in monotones as if trying hard to hold down his emotions. Sensing his discomfort, I did most of the talking at our first meeting, telling him about my experiences of being sexually molested and raped at a very young age. As I spoke, he stared at my face as if digesting every word. Finally, he started telling me his story.

"I don't remember a time when I wasn't molested," he said. "First it was my mother's boyfriend when I was only four. He did awful things to me for years. Then my uncle started in. Later, my older cousins took their turns." Tears were streaming down his cheeks, and he wiped his nose and eyes with his hands. "I thought there must be something wrong with me. I figured I was just born this way and had no choice. Men have always wanted me, and that was all I could ever be. But your story gave me hope. Can you help me?"

I smiled. "With God's help I can, but it's really up to you. Will you let God into your life so He can help you?"

Edmund looked doubtful. He shook his head. "God wants nothing to do with me. With all that's happened, I don't trust anyone. I'm gun-shy, and I can't change that."

"Then you're the perfect candidate," I said gently. "God really wants to show you just how much He loves you, Edmund. Have you ever read the gospels? Jesus surrounds Himself with the broken, the outcasts, the poor, the sick, the sinners—all ragamuffins," I said. I leaned toward my bookshelf, pulled out a paperback New Testament, and handed it to him. "Read the Gospel of Mark. It's the second book of the New Testament. Read it all week and then tell me what you've learned when we meet again."

Edmund read the Gospel of Mark; then he read the whole New Testament. After that, he read the whole Bible. Three or four times during our counseling sessions, he broke out in demonic manifestations, with spiritual forces throwing him into a fit and raging out curses at God. When this first happened, I was shocked and unsure of how to handle it. But the Holy Spirit spoke quietly to me, saying, "I have given you My authority to cast out demons." Focused, I calmly ordered the demons to leave and never come back. Edmund eventually became completely free of all demonic possession and was transformed into a caring, lovable man with an enormous heart to serve God.

"I want to be baptized," he told me one day. "Will you stand with me?"

"It'd be an honor," I said.

Years later, my friends in the ministry organized a huge gala for my sixtieth birthday. I was delighted and amazed to see over a hundred people in attendance. Edmund was the first to approach the microphone and offer a toast. He looked out over the crowd and smiled.

"If it hadn't been for Wynn taking the time to love me and guide me to Christ and freedom, I would probably not be alive today," he said. "Wynn, you helped to save my life." Then he raised his glass and said, "Wynn has become the father I've always hoped for. Because of your help and support, I've officially changed my last name. I'm a new creation in Christ, and I'm also your son, Edmund Thompson. Happy birthday, Dad!"

To say I was emotional is an understatement. I had no idea he was going to do that.

To this day, Edmund still keeps in close touch, and he still calls me Dad.

Edmund (now Benjamin) Thompson.

Speaking at my first Exodus Europe, Africa,
and Middle East Conference in France.

Returning to the Anglican church in the old city of Jerusalem,
Israel, as the keynote speaker teaching one of the first
Dysfunctional Families and Shame seminars
(now From Shame to Intimacy with Christ) in 2001.

At my first Exodus Europe, Africa, and Middle East Conference in France. Included in the picture are Frank Worthen, Anita Worthen, Graham Hazell, and Jonathan Hunter.

34

BATTLE OF THE VISAS

It was now 2003. The letter came on a Saturday. It looked official, sealed in a white envelope with a notice stamped in red ink: "From the Department of Home Affairs." I had received many notices from this bureaucracy since arriving in South Africa six years earlier, but this was the first with red letters on the envelope. It didn't appear to be one of the usual reminders that my work visa was about to expire. A sinking feeling came over me as I took the envelope inside and sat at the kitchen table.

"What now?" I said out loud, tearing open the envelope and unfolding the letter.

This is an official notice from the South African Department of Home Affairs hereby notifying you that your request for an extension on your work visa has been denied due to section 6458 of the Housing Code: No work visas shall be granted to individuals with a criminal record. You have fourteen days as of receiving this notice to file for a hearing or leave the country.

Leave the country? But this is my home. A sense of power-lessness overcame me. Why was this happening now when God was growing Restoring Wholeness in such amazing ways?

What was I supposed to do? I didn't have money for a lawyer. How would I fight this?

From the very beginning, remaining in South Africa as a missionary had been wrought with government roadblocks. I arrived in the country in 1996, two years after Nelson Mandela had become president, and much had changed for foreign visitors in the country. If I had arrived before Mandela had been elected, I could have easily applied and remained in the country on a permanent residence visa. However, Mandela's government made it more difficult. The only visa available to me was a three-month tourist visa. Serving as a missionary on a tourist visa meant that I had to reapply every three months. It went like this: After the first three months expired, I had to fill out all the necessary paperwork requesting a three-month extension. After that extension elapsed, I had to leave the country and apply for a new tourist visa. This was a very time-consuming, costly, and untenable situation for someone trying to build a ministry; I never knew how long I was going to be able to remain in the country. Through it all, I had to trust God to make a way if He wanted me to stay. And He always did, but it was never easy.

After a year of leaving and reentering the country on a tourist visa, Pastor Samuel in Stellenbosch offered to help. He suggested I apply for a ministerial license and then after that for a work visa, stating on the paperwork that I worked for him through his church. This, he said, would allow me to remain in the country for a longer period before having to file for an extension.

"But I don't work for you," I said. "I'm a volunteer. I'm not employed anywhere."

"Don't worry," Samuel said, waving away my concerns. "This is how it is done here. I'll fill out the paperwork stating you work for me. This will satisfy the government."

Because this seemed to be the only way I could stay in the country without constantly renewing my tourist visa, I went along with it, thinking this was God's way for me. And for several years, while I worked in Cape Town, I was noted in the paperwork as working under Pastor Samuel. Every few years or so, I'd get a notice stating that it was time for my work visa to expire. I never tried to hide anything about my criminal record from the authorities. They had all the information from the very beginning and never questioned it. Each time the expiration notice came in the mail, I'd take a trip back to Stellenbosch, and Pastor Samuel would sign the paperwork for the renewal. This is how I was able to stay in the country for nine years.

However, once the newly elected government assumed office after Mandela retired in 1999, the agency started enforcing stricter rules when granting visas. Government officials were instructed to thoroughly investigate the paperwork of current visa holders, and my criminal record caught their attention. Suddenly I became an "undesirable" to them, and they didn't want me in their country. By this time, I was leading a burgeoning ministry and had my own apartment, a car, and committed responsibilities. Everything was planned for what I would be doing for the next year in Restoring Wholeness, including speaking engagements, conferences, and counseling sessions. Although I had been training leaders and teachers to work with me in the ministry, we were still a long way from having someone qualified to lead in my place.

"I don't understand," I cried out to God, still holding the notice.

I was frustrated and angry, pacing back and forth in my kitchen. Finally, I threw my fists down on the counter and screamed at God until my voice grew hoarse. Exhausted, I slumped into a chair. It was then I heard the quiet voice of God: *I can take whatever you want to throw at Me.*

I was cut to the heart. How could I yell at God like that? I thought about the first time I had taken offense with God. It was when I was a youth leader in California, and I had assumed God wanted me to have the bowling alley building for youth concerts. No, it was more than an assumption; it was an expectation. I expected God to do *my* will because I thought He owed it to me for how hard I was working for Him and for the trauma I had suffered as a child. The same thing happened in Switzerland. I had fallen back into sin after becoming discouraged. I blamed God for not instantly answering my prayer. That was my excuse. I had expected God to give me a clear sign because I thought He owed me something.

The clarity of this realization surged through me like a wave. I remembered the nail-scarred hands of Jesus, pulling me from the pit when I was living in Bishop. How could I be so ungrateful, thinking God owed me anything? He had given me His very life so I could be redeemed. He had given me a new life close to Him.

Falling to my knees, I cried out, "Oh, Lord, I see what You're showing me. I've been sidetracked from the truth. You've done everything for me. You don't owe me anything. My life is Yours. I don't know what You're going to do about all this, but I'm okay with anything You want to do. Help me to trust You no matter what that means."

Not long after this, a good South African friend of mine heard about my situation and offered to help. When I answered the phone, I immediately recognized his voice.

"Wynn, you've been struggling with your visa situation long enough. God has spoken to me to help you get a proper lawyer and get this all sorted out. Don't worry. I'll take care of everything."

I said a silent prayer thanking God and rested in His provision.

A husband-and-wife team known in the Cape as being some of the best visa lawyers agreed to work with me. They questioned me for an hour and assured me that all would work out. However, they missed the deadline to get the paperwork filed, and I found out I was living in South Africa as an illegal alien the following Monday.

When I walked into the Home Affairs Office that morning, I thought I might be arrested. However, the officers pleasantly surprised me by being kind and understanding. They gave me a three-week extension to work things out. One of the special blessings during this visit was meeting Ina, who worked as a secretary in the office. Because I had to return there yearly and sometimes even monthly and weekly, Ina and I became friends. We talked more freely about my faith when we were the only two in the office. On one visit, I told her about my childhood trauma and shared with her how God had turned what the enemy meant for evil into good.

"This is why I'm in South Africa," I explained. "I'm here to help people caught up in addiction and abuse."

I could tell Ina felt safe with me because she began opening up about her own story and situation. During one of these visits, she confided in me that she had been sexually molested as a teenager. On another visit a few years later, she asked me to pray for her because she and her husband were in financial straits and were about to lose their home. She knew I was a Christian counselor and an ordained minister and often asked me about my faith.

I knew God was using me in Ina's life, but I had no idea to what extent and how it would affect my own situation.

⁓

Because the husband-and-wife lawyer team failed to do their job on my case, my supporters found and paid for a different attorney in Pretoria. This was an older gentleman who not only helped me to file the right paperwork, but also advised me to seek character references from friends and ministry partners all over the world. I had to get letters from the countries where I had ministered, proving my character was beyond reproach. It was amazing how many letters came in with glowing reports. I was humbled by their responses. It didn't take long for my lawyer to build a strong case on my behalf.

Then, in 2005, my lawyer forwarded me a letter from the South African Department of Home Affairs. This time, it was from the minister of Home Affairs, who declared my "undesirable" status lifted, allowing me to apply for a three-month visitor permit. This gave me the time I needed to reapply for another work visa.

After this victory, my lawyer in Pretoria retired and things seemed to be settled. I would return to the Home Affairs office each year for the next two years to renew my work visa without a hitch. Each time, I would see Ina and we'd have a nice visit.

However, in early 2007, things took a turn for the worst. I needed Pastor Samuel to sign the paperwork for my work visa extension, but for some reason, he wouldn't take my phone calls. I finally tried driving there to see him in person, but he wouldn't talk to me. I had no idea why he was acting so strange and couldn't think of anything I had done to cause offense. After making a few phone calls to some mutual friends, I discovered Samuel had had a falling out with the TRAILBlazers ministry, which his church had partnered with when the ministry relocated near the Cape. I can only assume Samuel wanted nothing to do with me because of my previous association with

TRAILBlazers. It was a nasty bit of business, and I was shocked and disheartened over it.

When the work visa expired, I was once again an illegal alien.

I was filled with trepidation as I drove to the Home Affairs office that Monday morning. Fortunately, Lenie, one of my Restoring Wholeness board members, came with me to pray and intercede in the car while I discussed my options with the officers inside.

I noticed Ina's changed appearance immediately when I walked in. Instead of wearing her work clothes, she was dressed in a Home Affairs uniform with a badge.

"What's happened to you?" I said with a big smile on my face.

Her eyes lit up at the sound of my voice, and she rushed over and hugged me. I was shocked. This kind of affection NEVER happens in a government building.

"I decided to take your advice," she said. "I gave all my issues to Jesus. And then God turned my life around! Last year I was promoted to an official position. If it wasn't for you giving me wise counsel, I don't think any of this would have happened."

"Praise the Lord!" I said. "That's awesome! What about your house?"

"God came to the rescue," she said. "Someone helped us with the finances and then I got this promotion."

I was so happy for her; I didn't want to break the mood by telling her about my struggles. But she seemed to know what was going on because she asked me if I was able to straighten things out.

"Unfortunately, my news is not as joyous as yours," I said.

After listening to the whole story, she said, "let me go see what I can do."

She returned ten minutes later and told me her supervisor had authorized her to write a letter, giving me another month to try to work things out. Then she wrote something down on a piece of paper and handed it to me. "I want you to go see this lawyer. He's very good. He's my personal lawyer."

I stood there with the paper in my hand, dumbfounded. But she didn't stop there. She called her lawyer and told him about my situation, asking him if he had time to see me that morning.

"His office is only a few blocks from here," she told me. "He said you can come by today."

When I left the office, I felt like I was floating. I climbed into the car and told Lenie the whole story.

"Praise God!" Lenie exclaimed. "Let's go see him now."

The lawyer greeted us when we walked in and asked us to sit down. He was in his late forties and listened quietly to my whole story. He agreed to help and told me exactly what to do. I would need to return to the United States for four months, then reapply for a three-month tourist visa. South Africa had just started issuing missionary visas, he said, so he would apply for one during my three-month stay on a tourist visa. I would just need to come up with 30,000 Rand ($2,034 US). This would cover my visa fine, my lawyer fee, and my airfare.

God had already moved so much on my behalf; how could I doubt He would provide the money? But it did seem like an awful lot, and my anxiety levels were going up.

You've been doing the wrong thing all along, a taunting voice rang in my head. *See? God isn't really with you. You're going to end up in jail.*

I knew better than to listen to that voice. When I got home, I sat in my chair and cried out to the Lord. "Father, I don't understand. But You are faithful."

I was surprised by the answer I received. Instead of telling me all was well, a thought came into my head, and I spoke it out loud: "I have to forgive."

Forgive? I thought. *Lord, is that You?*

But I knew it was. And I knew exactly what God was referring to. I was harboring resentment toward Pastor Samuel for refusing to see me and sign my paperwork. But resentment has no place in the Kingdom of Heaven, and God wanted me to forgive him.

I released it into God's hands and didn't take it back. All the money I needed came in a few days later. Forgiveness was the key.

35

THE ORCHESTRATION

Later that year, I was at home when my office manager called me.

"There's an email addressed to you from a Judi Sabin. Is that someone you know?"

I recognized the name immediately. It was the beautiful girl I had almost married in the '70s. Although I knew Sabin was her married name, I hadn't heard anything about Judi for over thirty years. I asked him to forward the email to me.

> Hi Wynn, Remember me? This is Judi. I found you by doing a Google search. It looks like you're doing very well. I am so pleased!
>
> My main reason for writing is to see how your mother is doing. I think of her often and was hoping to reconnect. Can you give me her contact information? I'd appreciate it.

So many years had passed, yet I could still imagine her voice as I read her words. I was eager to reconnect and quickly wrote back, breaking the news about Mom's death. Knowing she had married a pastor, I asked her about her family and described my own experience of coming back to God, participating in YWAM's missionary training, and starting Restoring Wholeness in South Africa.

I ended the email with this: "I'm so glad you contacted me because you're one of the last people I still need to ask to forgive me. I treated you very badly, and I'm so sorry. Can you forgive me?"

She wrote back a few days later: "Oh, Wynn, I forgave you years ago."

We corresponded a few more times after that. She told me her husband had passed away from a heart attack earlier that year, and she was living with her parents in Hemet, California. Her two adult sons were also in Southern California.

⁓

Looking back, I can see how God was orchestrating the next phase of my ministry by bringing both old and new friends from the United States into my life. In addition to Judi, there was also a young man named Brett Martin, who came to South Africa with Chi Alpha from the University of Arizona (UA) campus ministry in Tucson. As part of their ministry, Chi Alpha sends its leadership teams on worldwide missionary trips each summer. In 2007, the trip was to Timbuktu, Mali, where they were asked to teach and minister at a conference. When they arrived, they discovered the conference had been canceled and found themselves in the country with no outreach venue to participate in. They contacted Chi Alpha's headquarters, which reached out to several churches in South Africa to see if any had outreach opportunities for the group. A Swiss couple, Lars and Anina, who were coordinating an outreach ministry to homeless people in the Cape community, gladly responded to Chi Alpha's offer for help.

When Brett arrived, he became close friends with Lars and Anina and told them about his desire to reach those struggling with sexual brokenness.

"You need to meet Pastor Wynn," Lars said. "I'll introduce you."

It was a divine appointment. Both Brett and I knew God had brought us together for a reason, but Brett was only staying in South Africa for a few weeks. What was God up to?

Before he left, he said, "I'll raise the money so I can come back and sit and learn from you. I want to know more about what you do and how we can work together."

Because I needed to return to the United States to apply for the tourist visa, I planned some speaking engagements in several California churches and arranged with Brett and his pastor at Central City Assembly of God in Tucson, Arizona, to lead a two-day teaching conference. I would be staying with Brett at his home while there.

Before leaving, I contacted Judi and asked if she'd proofread the four-topic manual I had put together for the Tucson seminar. She hesitated. "I probably won't do a very good job because I usually get too involved in the content," she said. "But I'll try."

She had no idea just how involved she would become.

36

BACK TO THE STATES

The four months I stayed in Rancho Cucamonga, California, with my nephew Shawn and his family went by like a whirlwind. Judi came by to see me a few days after I arrived, and although thirty-five years had marred us with extra wrinkles, thinning hair, and additional weight, it mattered little.

I suggested we grab a bite to eat at a nearby Mexican restaurant, and she gladly agreed. Because it was early, we nearly had the place to ourselves. From the moment we sat down, we began filling each other in on our lives. First the chips and salsa came, and then our dinners were eaten, but we continued to visit. What I thought would be an hour-long dinner turned into a four-hour journey of discovery. Judi was no longer that innocent girl who idolized me. She was a strong, mature woman who had walked through her own paths of sorrow and joy. And her faith in God had stood the test of time with quiet fortitude and strength that only the scars of life can cultivate.

She pulled a printout of the seminar teaching I had

asked her to proofread from her purse and handed it to me. There were a few red markings on each page.

"I'm afraid I probably didn't do a very good job," she confessed. "I had no idea how deep this ministry went. I cried through the whole thing. After the first three lessons, I said to God, 'Okay, that's enough, Father.' When I saw the last lesson was on understanding same-sex attraction, I was relieved because I didn't think I had any connection to that issue. I thought it would be easier to read. But it hit me even harder! I didn't realize how this had affected you—or me. God spoke to me through the material, but I don't think I proofed anything. It proofed *me*!"

When Judi dropped me off at my nephew's house after dinner, we made plans to visit where we grew up and have a few more adventures together while I was in the States. I couldn't wait to see her again.

⁓

I had two speaking engagements along the Pacific Coast—one in Lompoc, a beach town in central California, and the other in Florence, Oregon. Judi had previously agreed to help her son move from Portland to Los Angeles, and she graciously planned her trip around mine so we could meet near Portland and visit with a mutual friend named Jeff Karlin from our youth group days. Jeff had been raised in the Jewish faith and had attended the youth meetings with a friend of his. Judi and I had been instrumental in leading Jeff to the Lord, and it was wonderful to see him still loving and serving God after all those years. We spent our time with him tasting cheese at the Tillamook Cheese Factory and then visiting the waterfalls in the Columbia River Gorge.

After Oregon, I flew to Tucson for the seminar with Brett and his pastor, Dave Ferrari. Their church met in an old two-story house on University Boulevard. Dave and his wife, Tori, had just started the church that year with a handful of college students and several homeless individuals. Dave and Tori lived primarily in the upstairs portion of the house, while the downstairs living room and dining room were dedicated to church services on Saturday evenings. Tori had also founded and ran Springboard, a Teen Challenge ministry for girls struggling with drug addictions. The Springboard girls lived together in Oro Valley, a community northwest of Tucson, but always attended church at the University house location. After each service, the Ferraris would serve dinner to all who wished to stay and fellowship.

In addition to the Thursday and Friday seminar, Pastor Dave asked me to preach at the Saturday evening service. I'm not sure how they got the word out, but the house was packed with people during all three days of the seminar. There were probably over a hundred people sitting in the living room, the dining room, and even on the stairs. Pastor Dave said it was the largest gathering his new church had seen thus far.

I was teaching about healthy boundaries and the dynamics of dysfunctional families, how to overcome sexual abuse, and how God can set us free from sexual addiction—a subject that was especially fascinating to the girls in Springboard. After the seminar was over, they begged Tori to bring me to their house in Oro Valley for further teaching the following Monday. I agreed to come and had barely started teaching them when they began firing questions at me. No one had ever spoken to them about this subject, and they were hungry to know more. The high level of interest from the attendees at both events did not go unnoticed by Tori, Dave, or Brett.

"There seems to be a real need for your ministry here," Dave told me over lunch the next day. "Have you ever thought about moving back to the States?"

I nearly choked on my food. "Have you ever been to South Africa?" I asked.

"No," he said.

"Well, if you had, you'd understand why I don't ever want to leave. It's a gorgeous place to live, and God has given me a successful ministry there."

Pastor Dave seemed undaunted by my reply. "You should pray about it," he said.

When Brett took me to the airport the following day, he unknowingly echoed Pastor Dave's words. But I wasn't interested.

"You know where I live and how much is going on," I told him. "I can't just pick up and leave."

Brett nodded but said, "Boy, we could sure use you here."

I didn't give their appeal a second thought as I flew back to LA. The very idea of it seemed ludicrous.

⁓

My last week in Rancho Cucamonga involved preparing to speak at the megachurch my nephew attended in Fontana. My nephew's wife had told a lady at their church about my ministry, which piqued the woman's interest because her son was battling with his sexual identity. Like many Christian parents in her predicament, she struggled with how to respond to him in Christ's love without condoning his behavior. She pressed the pastoral staff at her church to invite me to speak. The leadership responded by offering a half-day seminar where I would teach parents how to approach and respond to children in the gay lifestyle.

Since it was the last speaking engagement I would have before I returned to South Africa, I asked Judi to join me. When we arrived, about twenty-four people were sitting in a large classroom. Most were the parents of children who were struggling with their sexual identities and same-sex attraction. Before I started teaching, I told them my personal story.

"My journey to freedom in Christ has been a process. It's taken years. I became free from sexual addiction and homosexuality not from a program or counselor but through my relationship to Christ," I explained. "The more I came to know Him, the more I wanted to be like Him. I wanted to honor Him. Now my choice is to please Him for the sacrifice He made for me by dying on the cross. Does this mean all temptations are gone? Not at all. But He gives me the strength to make quality decisions, which gives me true peace. Everyone has a choice, and those choices have consequences—both good and bad. Through it all, God has been faithful in my life. I choose to honor Him and not my human desires. But I never condemn anyone. It's not my place. That responsibility belongs to God. I am definitely *not* God."

Then I turned the subject to the family and how important the parents' role is in encouraging strong identities in their children.

"My parents never talked about these things. Unfortunately, this is the norm, not the exception. Even today, most families don't talk about what really matters, only surface stuff." I looked around the room and saw troubled expressions on some of the faces gazing back at me. "We have to remember that children only imitate, while parents model. Parents need to watch and listen to their children. The responsibility we carry as adults can mean life or death to the identities of our kids. If they don't feel the freedom and safety to confide in you, then they won't confide."

The audience's response to my teaching was emotional. Many were outraged at the church in general, which had remained silent on same-sex attraction and sexual identity, giving no help or support to parents who were struggling with it in their homes. They were sorrowful, frustrated, and angry. Being in this ministry for over eighteen years had prepared me for their reactions. I knew the Holy Spirit was in charge, and this helped me to stay calm while I responded to their questions.

"Why hasn't this ever been taught before?" a woman asked one of the pastors attending the event. "I could have used this information years ago."

Seeing the need for more teaching, a few church leaders

spoke to me afterward about conducting more seminars, but I said, "I'm going back to South Africa tomorrow. Please contact me there, and I'll send you some information." Unfortunately, I never heard from them.

My visa now approved, I was yearning to return to my home and ministry in South Africa. Still, I was encouraged that some churches in the United States seemed to be open to this kind of ministry.

The hardest part about leaving was saying goodbye to Judi. When she dropped me off after the Fontana seminar, I hugged her, and she began to cry.

"I'm sorry," she said. "I don't know why I'm acting this way. I guess I don't want you to go."

What's this all about? I wondered. I had been working in the ministry and had chosen to be single and celibate for so long, I didn't even consider that Judi might have deeper feelings for me than friendship.

My family enjoying time together after my oldest nephew
Shawn's PhD ceremony.

37

A NEW CHAPTER

Returning to South Africa had a profound effect on me. Nothing seemed to be the same. My speaking schedule was full, and the South African government had just reinstated the missionary visa, which I had applied for, but I couldn't shake the feeling that something was about to shift.

Then I was invited into Pastor Anthony's church office and given some news. Restoring Wholeness was being asked to move out of the church office.

This blindsided me. I sat staring into my coffee mug, struggling to form the right words. "I'm not sure I understand," I finally said. "Do you need the office space for another ministry?"

"You're away a lot," the pastor explained. "And very few of the people involved with Restoring Wholeness attend our church anymore. We'd like to utilize the space in a way that will help to build our church body."

How could I protest? It wasn't like we were paying for

the space. Weary and feeling resigned, I stood up. "How soon would you like us to leave?" I asked.

"There's no huge hurry," he said. "If you can try to find a place so that you're moved out in a month or two, that should be fine."

We shook hands, and I thanked him for providing the office for as long as he did. I hoped I sounded as grateful as I ought to have felt. "We couldn't have done any of this without your support," I said.

When I got home, I tried to pray, but I didn't feel God's presence. *Lord, what are You up to now?*

By this time, losing the office should have been only a minor setback, but it had a huge impact on my state of mind. Nevertheless, I was disciplined and kept my focus on what was on my calendar—planning a two-month trip of speaking engagements in England, Scotland, and Switzerland, as well as my local schedule for training, counseling, and speaking events.

Through all of this, my thoughts kept going back to Judi and how she had cried when saying goodbye. We were Skyping every week now, and it was such a comfort to see her beautiful face and hear her voice. I missed her and found myself wishing she was there with me. I looked forward to our Skype visits like a kid anticipating Christmas.

It was during one of these visits when I experienced a deep sensation like butterflies swirling around in my stomach. *What's this?* I wondered. Looking at Judi through the laptop screen, I had a feeling I hadn't had before. It was the urge to protect her. *Oh my gosh, I'm in love with this woman. I never stopped loving her.* My previous rebellion into the homosexual lifestyle seemed so far away now, and God's true purpose and identity for my life just took another turn of clarity.

"Judi," I said into the microphone while peering at her on the screen, "do I have to get down on one knee?"

She shook her head, and I knew by the twinkle in her eye and the small grin on her face that she understood. "Oh no, don't do that," she said. "I'll marry you."

38

A NEW HOME

It's hard to pinpoint the moment when I knew God wanted me to move back to the States. There was no clear message from the Holy Spirit, but as soon as I proposed to Judi, I knew I would be leaving South Africa, even if it was only for a time.

I wondered why God would be calling me away then. Restoring Wholeness was thriving. I was booked solid for the next three months in South Africa and in Europe. I also knew Judi and I were supposed to be together; I knew there was an interest and a need for the Restoring Wholeness ministry in Tucson, and my heart was split. God had given me such a love for South Africa and its people; they had become family. I couldn't imagine saying goodbye.

Above all, I worried about Restoring Wholeness. What would happen to it after I left? I wanted a particular board member who had a fantastic personal testimony to accept the South African leadership role, but he and his wife were busy raising two children and working high-powered jobs. He didn't have time to lead the ministry. This was the reality. Restoring Wholeness had become so big that only a full-time position would be adequate to run it.

Our board held meetings to figure things out, and we finally settled on a decision. Curt Houser,[21] a fellow volunteer and leader in the ministry, offered to be my replacement. Curt had chosen to leave the homosexual lifestyle and was miraculously healed of AIDS. He had been with Restoring Wholeness for a few years and had often taught in support groups. He knew the material well. I was relieved he offered to take on the position, but I wondered if he was ready. I eased my mind by focusing on his training so the transition would be as smooth as possible.

All seemed to be going as well as could be expected until a few weeks before my departure, when Curt came over. A thin man in his thirties, he sank into my couch and avoided eye contact.

"What's up?" I asked.

He didn't answer right away but pressed his hands together under his nose. "I know I should have said something earlier," he said slowly, "but I thought I could shake this feeling."

"What do you mean?"

"I can't do this," he blurted out. "You need to find someone else."

I was shocked; something wasn't right. "But you told me you wanted to do this. I don't have time to train anyone else. What do you expect me to do?"

---

21   Curt's real name has been changed for his privacy.

"I don't know," he said flatly.

I sat in silence for some time, trying to control my emotions so I wouldn't say anything I'd later regret.

"Okay. I hear you," I said. "But since you're telling me this at the last minute, will you at least agree to be the acting leader until we can replace you? That will give us some time to find and train someone else."

He shook his head. "You can't train anyone when you're not here."

He had a point, but I had to try. "The board will help. We'll find a way. If not, I'll raise the money and come back to train someone. But I need you to agree to do this for a year. Can you promise me that much?"

Curt blew air through his fingers. "Okay, but definitely no longer than a year. Six months would be better."

"I'll talk to the board," I said. "Just keep things afloat. That's all I ask."

"Okay. I guess."

If I had been uncertain about leaving before, I was now downright anxious about it. But what could I do? Judi and I had pooled our resources and had already paid for the wedding. Most of my things were packed and ready to be shipped, and my plane ticket was purchased. I would have to trust God for the ministry and do what I could from a distance until I could return.

Lord, I prayed, *why can't things be easier and run more smoothly?*

I was busy that last month before leaving. I spoke in churches around the Cape every Sunday, and my counseling schedule was booked as I worked to bring closure to those God had entrusted to me. It was a hectic time, and I wondered if I'd ever complete everything that had to be done. Thank God for giving me the strength and wisdom to see it through.

I spent my last days in South Africa talking over the details of our plan with my board, letting them know what Curt and I had discussed and asking them to help him as much as possible with the administrative duties. They agreed to keep me informed on all that transpired.

This gave me more peace about the situation. Every time I started feeling anxious, I would remind myself that Restoring Wholeness was God's ministry and not mine. If God wanted me to take it to the United States, then I needed to trust Him.

I also tried to focus on what I was transitioning into. I was about to become a married man. Who would have thought that I would be the husband of a beautiful Christian woman who had also been one of the best friends I had ever known—especially now that I was in my sixties? What a wonder!

The day of my departure felt surreal. As I was going through airport security, my mind was focused on the year to come. What would it be like to be a husband—to take care of Judi and be her companion into our old age? Would I be up to the task? How would I support her as a missionary?

My mind was so preoccupied with these thoughts I hardly noticed the check-in procedures at the airport. As I walked onto the plane, I wondered what the future would hold. Would Judi and I be staying in the United States or returning as a couple to continue ministering in South Africa? Somewhere in the recesses of my mind, I knew that was my ultimate hope. But it had to be God's will. I had to trust Him.

39

THE REBOOT

After my plane landed at the Ontario International Airport on a Tuesday evening, I stopped in the airport restroom and looked at myself in the mirror. The long plane trip had left dark circles under my eyes and a cowlick at the back of my head. This wouldn't do, I thought, running cold water over my hands and smoothing down my hair. Then I brushed my teeth and splashed cold water across my face. I wanted to look my best for what was coming next.

My niece, Sherri, and Judi were waiting for me in the baggage area. I could see them as I came down the escalator, and my heart began to beat faster. I walked briskly up to Judi, went down on one knee, and drew out a small box from my pocket. Opening the box, I pulled out a diamond ring made especially for her in South Africa.

"I'd like to ask you a question," I said, smiling.

Judi laughed. "What? Here?"

Although I had already proposed to her over Skype, I felt it only proper to do it face to face with a ring. I had prepared this with my niece ahead of time, and she was taking pictures. A group of people near us was watching as if sensing the importance of the moment.

Taking Judi's hand in mine, I said, "Please, marry me?"

Tears welled up in Judi's eyes, and she nodded her head. Her beautiful smile was all I needed as confirmation. I slipped the ring onto her finger, stood up, and embraced her.

⁓

Before we were married, Judi and I had decided to settle in Tucson, mainly because Pastor Dave at Central City Assembly said he was interested in having Restoring Wholeness as one of the ministries at the church. Judi applied for an employment position in Tucson with the same company for which she worked in California, and we spent a few weeks looking around for a place to live. Then we traveled up to Bishop, where we were married by my youngest nephew, Patrick, who had become a pastor.

Surrounded by family and friends, the ceremony took place in a beautiful park at the foot of the Sierras. We stood near a mountain stream as Judi's oldest son walked her down the aisle. I was a mess when it was my turn to say my vows. Tears rolled down my face, and I stuttered as I spoke while looking in Judi's eyes. I couldn't believe this was finally happening. The last month in South Africa and the first few months back in California and Tucson were a blur. After my rebellious and sinful life, how was it I could be blessed by God with Judi as my wife? Our marriage was ordained by God; I was certain of it.

Several of my friends from South Africa and Switzerland flew to California to attend our wedding. One of these friends handed us a check for two thousand dollars during the reception. "For your next trip to South Africa," he said.

After he left, I told Judi, "This is a miracle. I didn't know how I would have the money to get back to South Africa to work out the ministry's issues." My friend at the wedding didn't even know about the need. God had come through . . . again!

After the reception, we spent the night in a nice bed-and-breakfast inn. The next morning, Judi received a very encouraging email from the owner of the company in Tucson where she had applied for a job. She was offered a position. God was in control and making a way for us to live in Tucson.

After saying goodbye to family and friends, we drove to Las Vegas for a two-day honeymoon. When we returned to Tucson, everything seemed to be going smoothly until only half of my shipment from South Africa arrived. Instead of the other palate of furniture, I received a notification that it had been water damaged and sent back. I made many calls to the shipper in South Africa, with no results. Although the shipment was insured, I was never compensated for the loss. I was swindled by a "Christian" moving company. I asked God to forgive them and let it go. They were only things, after all, and things can be replaced.

As disheartening as this was, it was nothing compared to what happened next.

Curt was not returning my phone calls or emails. I contacted the Restoring Wholeness board members, but they were also unable to connect with him. When the ministry's bank account was drained, the only explanation I received was that Curt had taken it as his salary for the work he had done. I learned later that Curt had found a church that proclaimed homosexuality as acceptable to God. He returned to that lifestyle, taking a few others in the Restoring Wholeness group with him. I tried to reach out to them because I loved them all dearly and wanted the best for them. I had no judgment in my heart, only sadness about their animosity toward me—especially because we had been such close friends. Even so, I didn't hold any bitterness toward them. Everyone must make their own choices and be responsible for those choices.

My heart was broken. The ministry was teetering on the verge of collapse, and I felt completely helpless to save it. A young man named Cyril, who was working in the office with Curt when he left the ministry, graciously helped to keep things going, but I needed to get back there to see if I could find someone to take over the leadership position before all was lost.

Me and Brett Martin on one of our early-morning prayer walks, 2010.

Favorite photo taken in Bodie, California, just before our wedding. Overseas guests (left to right): Corinne Fehr, Francois Bonnet, Simon Dickenson, me and Judi, Laurance-Nicole Fehr, and my best man, Chris Ely, June 2009.

*Judi walking down the aisle with her oldest son,
Mike, at our wedding in 2009, Bishop, California.*

One of our wedding photos.

My brother, Brian, and his wife, Kay, June 2009.

Our wedding family photo. From left to right: Rachel Thompson, Arrisa Thompson, Sherri and Shawn Thompson, Hannah Thompson, Brian Thompson, Judi, Patrick Thompson, Wynn, Kay Thompson, Ida Williams, and Greta Thompson.

40

UNCOMFORTABLE
RESTORATION

Due to Judi's work situation, we had to wait a year before returning to South Africa. We used the money given to us at our wedding to help pay for the trip, which we called a second honeymoon. However, there was little time for rest and sightseeing because my schedule was booked with speaking engagements and meetings. One close friend even gave us two days and nights at a five-star hotel, but I was so busy I couldn't relax and enjoy myself—not even for those two days. Poor Judi put up with it, but I'm afraid it wasn't much of a honeymoon for her either.

Being a widow, Judi understood much more about the give and take of marriage than I did. I didn't even realize how inconsiderate I was being until one evening she asked me to consider her enjoyment as well. Although Judi knew about, and agreed to the speaking engagements and meetings I had planned, I knew she was right and apologized. I told her the next time we went to South Africa, we would have a real honeymoon.

"Oh no you don't," she said, laughing. "If and when we go on a real honeymoon, it won't be to South Africa or anywhere else where you're ministering. It'll be somewhere you've never been."

Judi is a wise woman.

I wasn't successful in finding a leadership replacement for Restoring Wholeness during my three weeks in South Africa. Everyone was either too busy or not suitable, and three weeks was not enough time to find the right person. One young man named Daniel came forward and offered to help where he could. It was his way of showing his appreciation for the help I had given him when I first moved Restoring Wholeness to Atlantic Christian Assembly. I knew him to be a trustworthy person who loved the Lord, but I also knew how busy he was with a young wife, three small children, and another one on the way. He neither could have nor should have tried to devote all his efforts toward the ministry. Still, I was touched by his offer and told him so.

~

Becoming a husband so late in life has been an enormous blessing, but it has also been a huge adjustment and challenge. It has opened my eyes to some things about my personality I probably should have discovered earlier in life but missed out on. But God has a way of bringing these things to the surface at just the right time, usually when we share our lives with others.

As demonstrated by our honeymoon experience, I realized I can often become too focused on a singular vision, and I needed to widen it to include Judi. While we had both changed quite a bit since the 1970s, when we were young and dating, we still had some narcissistic tendencies to overcome. When we were young, Judi and I used to spend hours preening ourselves before leaving on a date. We laugh about that now.

Later, when I was living as a single adult for so many years while running a ministry, my only focus was the ministry. But now that I was married, I found my priorities needed to shift. Suddenly, it wasn't just about me and what I was doing for God. There was another person in the equation who needed to be considered over my needs and even over the ministry. This was not an easy lesson for me to learn.

Adjusting to marriage, while coming to terms with what was happening to Restoring Wholeness in South Africa, nearly sank me emotionally. Because I felt powerless to prevent the dissolution of the ministry in South Africa, I tried refocusing my efforts in Tucson. Brett and others joined me to form a group for men who struggled with same-sex attraction. This was fulfilling because I was able to help several people, but I wasn't being invited anywhere to speak.

For the first time since I left the country for Switzerland in 1992, I found myself with little to do. The ministry seemed to be sinking beneath a cultural imperative that claimed homosexuality was not only normal but something to be celebrated. I realized that if Restoring Wholeness was going to survive in the United States, I had to start the ministry again from the ground up, but this time it would be in a climate of opposition. Sadly, this opposition has come from the church as well as popular culture.

Through it all, I was trying to keep busy and cover up my sense of hopelessness, especially from Judi.

One day while watching an old movie on TV, the phone rang. Judi was at work, and I tried to ignore it. *Just go away*, I thought. But something nudged me to turn off the TV and answer.

It was Brett. He said I had been on his heart and mind. "Ah . . . okay," I said slowly, letting the words roll out of my mouth.

"What's going on with you?" Brett asked.

I hemmed and hawed and then finally admitted, "I'm not good. I feel frustrated and irritated all the time." Finally admitting this out loud to someone caused me to break out in a sweat, and I wiped my forehead with my hand.

"It sounds like you might be depressed," Brett said gingerly.

That suggestion got my attention. He was right. Most of my days involved being curled up on the sofa, stuffing my face with popcorn while watching movie after movie. It was a mindless way to distract myself from an overwhelming sense of sadness, stress, and loss. There was an empty, nasty feeling deep in my core that would not go away, and I felt agitated and angry most of the time.

How did I not see I was depressed? I had spent the last thirteen years counseling and speaking to troubled people who were often suffering from depression. I knew the signs well but had been blind to my condition.

Brett said he suspected this and decided to read up on the subject. He was convinced I had been bombarded with stressful situations that had sent me into a tailspin. This made sense. I had experienced a lot of stress since coming back to the States. After hanging up, I began to practice what I preached and made a list.

Some of the most stressful situations humans experience are:

- changing employment
- making a major move
- getting married
- having a baby
- coping with death

At first, I thought I had experienced at least three of these. I had lost my ministry in South Africa—very much like a death. Check. I made a major move back to the United States. Check. I had gotten married. Check.

Within an hour, I came up with two more: changing jobs and birthing a new ministry.

I called Brett back, and we prayed together over the phone. I humbled myself and cried out, "Lord, do what You need to do in me to heal me. I want Your joy to fill me so I can carry on with what You have called me to do." It was the breakthrough I needed. Sometimes God heals us as part of a process over time. Other times, He does things quickly. Praise God this was one of those times!

As for South Africa, I was finally able to surrender it to God. This has been one of the hardest lessons I've ever had to learn. Even if God uses us to start a ministry, it doesn't mean we can claim ownership over that ministry. It all belongs to Him. Even so, my heart remains with the people of South Africa. They are like family to me, and I am so grateful for the time I was able to spend there.

Over the past several years, God has transformed me into a more positive and encouraging man, helping me to focus more on Jesus and less on myself. It's such a waste of time getting lost in negativity because it takes us away from God's presence and His purpose. It locks us into the dark prison of our insecurities and shortcomings.

One night I had a dream of being trapped in a dark, horrible-smelling pit. The darkness was so thick I couldn't breathe. Then I saw the nail-scarred hand of Jesus reaching down and pulling me out to safety. The Lord completely washed me clean from head to toe. In place of the heaviness, I was flooded with lightness and joy. I knew I was free from depression.

I realized then more than ever that if we do not understand the pit we are in, we cannot appreciate the Lord, who reaches down to lift us out and save us.

From that point on, God has made a way for me to grow and become what He has purposed me to be here in America. Humble transparency has been the key.

Once I accepted that things were different and leaned more on God for direction and peace, my life began to change. Instead of covering up my feelings of hopelessness and insecurity with Judi, I began communicating and praying with her. My relationship with Judi has grown in ways that have been an encouragement and strength for both of us.

Invitations started coming in to speak at conferences overseas, especially in the Ukraine, where there is a great interest in helping those in sexual brokenness. Doors also opened in Switzerland, and many churches in South Africa requested weeklong teachings focused on the topics in our Restoring Wholeness Support Group manual.

The ministry in the United States now has a strong and creative board of directors. With doors opening overseas, our team in America decided it was time to update our manual, which was originally written in 2000 by our South African team. It has also been translated into Russian, Ukrainian, and partly in French.

Although Restoring Wholeness still ministers to those seeking help who struggle with same-sex attraction, our focus is to help all seek help from addiction—relationally, socially, and sexually. We only serve those who want our help, and we do not coerce people away from lifestyle choices. Rather, we disciple them into a closer relationship with Jesus. It is through this relationship with Christ that people find transformation. Our program works well for those who have been abused or addicted, families who have been broken under the weight of dysfunctional shame, relational idolatry (or emotional dependence), and many other related issues. We pray people find the help they need, and we are eager to help where we can.

We offer no judgments, only support and help. If God is not at the center of all we are, there is no hope. But hope is our fiber; it is at the core of everything we do in our personal lives, our marriages, our work, and our ministry.

God must get all the glory for everything He has done in our lives. We pray He will restore wholeness in your life as well.

Speaking at Life Church, pastored by Chris Swart,
Somerset West in the Cape, South Africa.

Epilogue

BLESSED HOPE

Thank you for taking the time to read my story. I do not pretend that it typifies all those who feel trapped in sexual brokenness and addiction. In counseling people over thirty years, I have discovered there are numerous paths that lead to brokenness. However, I have also seen that we all share a common thread: We have faulty belief systems that start with misconceptions. In other words, we believe lies about ourselves, or others, or both. And these lies grow and become influencers in our poor decisions.

There is only one way to stop believing lies. They must be exposed to the truth. The good news is that God is in the lie-exposing business! He is the truth, and He desires to walk with us and show us our dysfunction so that we can become free to live an abundant and fruitful life in Him. This process might take a lifetime—in fact, it most certainly will—but what a reward awaits us, not only in this life, but also in the life to come!

Won't you join me?

*Brett and me in Kiev, Ukraine, at CBN studios, holding a
three-day live on-air seminar on issues of sexual brokenness
with Teen Challenge National leader Sergey Glushko and
YWAM leader Alyona Yukhymchuk, plus many other Ukraine
and Russian ministry leaders.*

Being interviewed on CBN Television in the Kiev, Ukraine.

*Judi and I with one of my mentors in YWAM, Jim Isom,
and his wife Judy. Jim is creator of
Dysfunctional Families and Shame.*

*The first live broadcast of a three-day conference
on CBN Kiev, Ukraine. The conference covered teachings
on all areas of sexual brokenness.*

From left to right, front row: Judi; great-niece Arissa; sister-in-law Kay; great-niece Rachel holding her sister Hannah. Back row (left to right): Wynn; Greta Thompson with her husband and Wynn's youngest nephew, Patrick; brother Brian; and oldest nephew, Shawn, and his wife, Sherri Thompson.

Appendix

THE CRISIS OF SEXUAL IDENTITY

Adapted from "The Crisis of Sexual Identity in Today's Family and Church," by Wynn Cameron Thompson, January 2003, *Big God, Big Life*

I once read a story about a man in England who was walking down a street and passed a tattoo parlor. In the window were pictures of some of the tattoos being offered. One tattoo, in particular, caught his eye. It declared in bold black letters: "Born to Lose." The image stopped him in his tracks. How could anyone want those words branded onto their skin? His curiosity got the better of him, and he stepped into the shop.

An old Chinese man stood behind the counter. He went up to him and asked, "Excuse me, but I just have to ask . . . do people really go for that tattoo, 'Born to Lose'?"

The old Chinese man replied, "Yes."

Shocked, he asked, "But why would anyone do that?"

The old man just looked at him and answered very seriously, "Before tattoo on body, tattoo on mind."

The crisis in man's identity, as well as his sexuality, must start somewhere. Most of us have managed to ignore, hide, or completely deny the innermost parts of our being. Our struggle as men has not come from one experience but several. From the day we were born and dressed in blue, influences from our family, friends, and society have dictated and created our present-day crisis, many times without our being aware of it. We have learned to hide rather than deal with the crisis in our identity. Our parents model a particular way of dealing with our crisis, and we as children have accepted it as truth. We have learned to shift the blame onto someone else, a trait inherited from Adam and Eve back in the Garden of Eden:

> The man said, "The woman whom you gave to be with me, she gave me fruit of the tree, and I ate." Then the LORD God said to the woman, "What is this that you have done?" The woman said, "The serpent deceived me, and I ate." (Genesis 3:12–13, ESV)

Children are great imitators but terrible perceivers. In other words, they don't know how to read between the lines. For children—or anyone, for that matter—to perceive, there must be clear communication. Many of us have grown up in homes where there was little or no communication between parents and children. The phrase "children should be seen and not heard" has condemned children to a life of silence and shame. It teaches them that what they feel and think has no value, and this belief is carried over into their adult lives.[22] This is a great pity because, as David Seamands says, "We all need an environment where we feel our needs are met because of who we are and not because of what we do."

In the church of today, we leaders and members have found ourselves secretly struggling with issues because we're afraid and ashamed to open up to each other for prayer. This is contrary to the blueprint laid out in scripture, which tells us:

Confess to one another therefore your faults (your slips, your false steps, your offenses, your sins) and pray [also] for one another, that you may be healed and restored [to a spiritual tone of mind and heart]. The earnest (heartfelt, continued) prayer of a righteous man makes tremendous power available [dynamic in its working]. (James 5:16, Amplified)

Having said this, we cannot confess to another person unless there is trust, and trust doesn't come easily. We must know the person over a long period, testing their integrity on small issues before we can launch out into the deeper matters of the heart. Two-way communication and vulnerability are essential for building that trust, and even then, you may find there are very few people you can trust with the issues of your heart.

The integrity of men today has been weakened by our human history of silence, denial, and fear. I believe the deepest root of our crisis is a break in the relational bonds

---

22 Dysfunctional Families and Shame teachings, Rev. James Isom.

within the family, producing a lack of affirmation and a great lack of a sense of belonging. Many times, this is subtle and unseen in the initial stages. Nevertheless, when it happens, it produces insecurity that can, and many times does, have a profound effect on adolescence. It also has a profound effect on a person's sexual identity in the family and the Church.

Security

The security of a child depends on a three-way bond: mother to child, father to child, and the often overlooked and neglected bond of father to mother. Children are always observing their parents. As Jesus said:

> *My Father is always at his work to this very day, and I, too, am working. I tell you the truth, the Son can do nothing by himself; he can only do what he sees his Father doing, because whatever the Father does the Son also does. For the Father loves the Son and shows him all he does. Yes, to your amazement he will show him even greater things than these that all may honor the Son just as they honor the father. He who does not honor the Son does not honor the Father who sent him. (John 5:16–23)*

Any disconnection in the triangle of mother, father, and child will produce insecurity in the child. Whether the disconnection is real or only perceived by the child, the results can be, and many times are, the same. The way he or she reacts to disturbance and confusion in the family unit (whether large or small) can affect the child.

These insecurities in the family result in mental and emotional confusion as to where the children fit in, how they should act, what their behavior should be toward the opposite sex, and so on. Confusion about these questions often results in fear, mistrust, uncertainty, and possible shame. In turn, these reactions can prevent children from interacting normally with people of both genders—an interaction that would normally help build their confidence and interpersonal skills.

What is not communicated clearly can easily be misunderstood, and the child receives a completely different message than that which was originally intended. However, in dysfunctional families, what is acted and spoken out in front of the child is exactly what was intended. The message is equally damaging regardless of which way it comes into the child's mind.

I was raised in a solid Christian home. My father and mother were incredibly involved in our local church, using their talents in every possible way. I remember attending almost every church service, crusade, and youth meeting. My parents were devout Christians who loved the Lord with all their hearts. I remember hearing their prayers, and I know they prayed every day for my brother and me.

Nevertheless, I was sexually molested several times during my childhood, and I was never able to tell my family what happened. There was an unspoken understanding in our family that we should only talk about the good things, so I felt trapped by my fear, guilt, and shame. I felt powerless, used, and betrayed, and I lost my sense of dignity and worth both inside and outside the family.

From that point on, I always felt inferior to others and had a deep conviction that I was unlovable. This is a common reaction for all victims of abuse, regardless of what degree of abuse they have suffered.

In my case, the abuse was perpetrated by a group of neighborhood boys and later by a twenty-five-year-old woman in our church and a man in a city park near our home. The first time it happened, I felt guilty, afraid, and ashamed. The second time it happened, I felt the same fear and shame but also loved the attention and the physical feeling associated with what had happened. The woman in my church did not rape me but touched me in inappropriate ways. The difference between rape and molestation is that those who molest usually do it from a twisted form of love, whereas a rapist is generally acting with the motivation of control, rage, or revenge.

When my parents found out what had happened with the woman at our church, my father confronted me and told me, "Get down on your knees and pray for forgiveness." I did not fully understand what was happening, but I did what he asked. At that moment, I felt alienated from my father's love because, in his opinion, I had allowed this to happen. As a result, I felt more fear, confusion, and shame. My dad felt dirty about what had happened and felt the reputation of the family was ruined. The only solution he could think of was to get cleansing and forgiveness—and in his mind, since I was the one involved, it was my duty to confess.

Because of this, I came to understand that sex with

women was bad, and to have any sexual feelings at all was a sin. Poor communication had led to this wrong perception of the world, and the shame for me was overwhelming. As a child and a teenager, I had no way to express what I was thinking or feeling. It was only much later in my adult years that I was able to talk with a counselor and begin to understand the train of events that had so distorted my sexual identity. Yet even as adults, we find it hard to express ourselves whether or not we have been molested or raped.

As a child, all I knew was that what I experienced with that woman felt good. Yet, at the same time, I experienced shame, guilt, and fear. When God created sexuality in mankind, He never intended the pleasure of sexuality to be mixed with shame and fear. Sexuality was intended as one of God's greatest gifts to mankind, but when sin entered the equation, the purity of the gift was destroyed, resulting in pain and confusion for many.

At the age of eleven, I experienced the awakening of sexual feelings within me, and the real struggle began. I had no idea how to handle these powerful feelings. In cases like mine, I've come to believe that parents must surround their children and make them feel safe and not guilty for what happened to them. I was large for my age and had mostly grown up around adults, so my demeanor was that of an older teenager, even at the age of eleven. However, this was in no way a justification for the abuse, and in no way was I at fault. The responsibility for the abuse always lies with the older child, teenager, or adult, who knows exactly what they are doing. At all times, it is imperative to reassure the child, as many times as necessary, that the abuse was not their fault.

Years later, when I was in Switzerland serving as a missionary with Youth with a Mission (YWAM), I met a young Swiss man, and we became very close friends. One night as we sat overlooking Lake Geneva, we began to talk. As I opened up to him and explained how my past related to the direction in which God was leading me, he shared with me that during his teens, he was, at times, suicidal. I asked him the reason for it, and he did not know. However, as I continued to share the story of my abuse, he gasped and said, "I just remembered something." He then began to share with me how as an eleven-year-old, he had gone to the cinema alone. As he sat there watching the movie, a man came to sit beside him and began sexually molesting him. "How did you feel?" I asked my friend. His head drooped as a cloud of shame came over him. He, too, had experienced mixed feelings; he felt guilty and ashamed, yet at the same time the physical feelings were good—in fact, rather exciting. I said to him, "Isn't it strange that two extremely different feelings can be experienced at the same time? God was the One who created those good feelings, not the devil. The devil can't create anything except confusion." The experience this young man and I went through was not in God's original plan for our lives. We were victims of the sinful choices of other people.

Many children find it difficult to accept that the abuse was not their idea or their desire. Why is this? Most children come to believe that they wanted the abuse to happen or that it was their fault for simply being there at the time of the abuse. Not only that, but all children have a deep hunger for love and attention. We all need to be wanted or to feel important, attractive, and valued by others. We also have a great need to feel safe and provided for. In most cases, a molester will play on these felt needs, talking to the children and answering their questions, making them feel important, and showering them with gifts. In this way, they fill the need for love and attention in the child, winning their trust and cooperation.

When a husband and wife come together in marriage and produce a child, the first and foremost responsibility is to meet that child's basic emotional and physical needs— and to meet them *unconditionally*. This is an exact reflection of our Father God's role in our lives. A parent would never say to a four-year-old, "Now that you can walk and talk, it's time to get a job so you can pay for your room and board." Yet many parents make extremely high demands of their children. When performance is not up to their standards, parents often withhold some of those most basic legitimate needs as a form of punishment. This is a mistake; legitimate needs should never be withheld from the child. However, this method of child-raising is often passed down from one generation to the next, increasing the sense of mistrust and insecurity from a young age.

If parents never talk about sex with their children, the child can come to believe that sex is dirty, embarrassing, or shameful. Sex is done in the dark and must be kept secret.

This cloak of obscurity only aids the abuser, who often tells the child that the abuse must be kept secret. Usually, the molester is a friend or family member, and those who molest generally don't physically hurt the child. The spiritual and emotional devastation they bring is another matter entirely.

Rejection by family members or friends, whether real or imagined, can also make a child more vulnerable to abuse. It is important to guard against those messages of rejection.

Children are also taught to respect and obey their elders without question, particularly spiritual authorities in the church. This, too, is a danger.

Children have an innate sense of when something is not right; parents should gently make them aware of the dangers of inappropriate touching and give them ways to handle these situations should they arise.

Safeguard Your Child Against Abuse

In my years of counseling, I've discovered two effective strategies that can help prevent your child from being molested. First, you should open up to them and talk about real issues. Give your children a healthy view of sex. Second, teach your children that they have the right to say *no* over what happens to their bodies and give them strategies for getting out of an awkward or dangerous situation.

Sexual abuse occurs when an older or more knowledgeable child or adult uses a child for sexual pleasure. The abuse often begins slowly and increases over time. Use of physical force is seldom necessary as children are naturally trusting and dependent and want to please others to gain love and approval. Children are also taught not to question authority.

After talking with many men concerning their own life experiences, I have learned that there are more male victims of sexual abuse in childhood than most realize. Many were molested by other boys their age or a little older. In cases where boys are sent to boarding school and required to live in a dormitory, many have experienced one, two, or more occasions of molestation. Some might call it play or experimentation, but the pain and confusion in later years prove otherwise. Later in life, some are driven to "perform" in heterosexual relationships to "prove their manhood." Others act out a drive toward same-sex relationships. Sexual addictions are a result of this type of compounded brokenness, which, in many cases, can lead to broken relationships.

Many others have been molested by women. Most boys who experience this type of molestation create a mask of denial over the event. I used to boast that when I was eleven, I had a twenty-five-year-old woman. Yet I was denying even to myself that this woman stole my virginity and my childhood from me. After the molestation, all I could think of was sex and how to get it. My school days were ruined, my grades fell, and I could not concentrate on my schoolwork. Within days of the abuse, I began to masturbate compulsively as a way of covering the pain I felt. To me, it was a warm, fuzzy security blanket that nobody could take from me. However, the problem with addictive behavior is that it never satisfies for long—it always leaves us longing for more.

In my case, the pain and confusion were never really addressed, and a year later, when a man approached me intending to molest me, I fell into the clutches of homosexuality without any struggle. I wanted the attention and love of my father and was longing for his masculine affirmation. Of course, my father had not really rejected me, but this was the message I took from his response to the abuse. It was my perception. The message received may not have been the message intended, but because the truth was not revealed through clear communication, the lie took hold, and I reaped a harvest of pain and confusion. From that point on, my life became more and more difficult, and I accepted *abnormal* sexual behavior as normal in my life.

Thankfully, most men do not experience this degree of trauma as they grow up. Yet many do experience rejection from their fathers at different levels, which creates a sense of disconnection from their father, who is the true source of their masculinity.

Frank Worthen, one of the founders of Exodus International, puts it this way:

A male child has certain needs that only his father can fulfill. The same is true of the female child with her mother. A male child's needs can be summed up in three words—strength, power, and protection. The male role is to initiate and the female role is to respond. These are to be the governing traits, although there will be some crossover from time to time; it is not unusual for males to respond and for females to initiate.

The male child needs to develop an active rather than passive personality. He must become a risk-taker. Under his father's covering, he feels free to explore his world and learn by trial and error. The strength, power, and protection of his father make this possible. He enjoys his relationship with his father, knowing that his father desires him to possess these traits for himself, rather than always being dependent on his father for them. These good feelings about his father transfer into love, affirmation, and a sense of belonging. He is secure in his father's identity and accepts that identity for himself.[23]

Blessing Your Child with Security

A family blessing on a child begins with meaningful touch—a hug or a pat on the shoulder. It continues with a spoken message of high value, a message that pictures a special future for the individual being blessed and gives an active commitment to seeing that future come to pass.[24]

Jesus Christ has this type of relationship with His Father; God spoke a very public blessing over His Son Jesus in the waters of baptism: "This is my son, in whom I am well pleased" (Matthew 3:17).

It took me years to realize that my search was not really for sexual fulfillment but genuine intimacy. *Oxford's Dictio-*

---

23 Frank Worthen, *Helping People Step Out of Homosexuality*, 1995.
24 Dysfunctional Families and Shame teachings, Rev. James Isom.

nary describes intimacy as "close familiarity or friendship; closeness" as well as "closely acquainted; familiar, close; essential and intrinsic." We are all designed to relate to another person who sees us at the deepest level and still loves and accepts us for who we are. I was searching for the elements of parental love in another male because I felt I had not received them from my father. Much of my homosexual search was an attempt to find strength, power, and protection from a male figure; the same is true for many other men.

Again, in the words of Frank Worthen:

> The female child also needs an identity trans-fer, but of a much different nature. A desire to be protected is normal and good. She should develop such trust in men through her father that she looks forward to having her special protector. She must come to see the female role as desirable, mother-hood as rewarding, and find dignity in serving. She develops wisdom quite differently from the male. She must not see the female role as degrad-ing and humiliating. She must thank God that He made her a female.
>
> The father is also very significant to his daugh-ter. In affirming her, loving her unconditional-ly, and approving of her femininity, he prepares her for healthy heterosexual development. As he expresses his love for her, and as she witness-es a strong bond of love between her father and mother, she perceives the goodness of the hetero-

sexual relationship. For both girls and boys, therefore, the father must provide stability and security. I was told a true story of a father who, on his arrival home, was met by his wife, who told him that his daughter was having a period for the first time. His wife told him that the daughter was up in her room crying and refusing to talk to anyone. The father went to his daughter's room and found her withdrawn and curled up on her bed. He went over and sat on the edge of the bed and said to her, "Honey, I'm so proud of you. Today you have become a woman. I want you to go and put on your finest dress because I'm taking you out to dinner." He then took her out to a fine restaurant and treated her like a queen.[25]

When sons and daughters have no firm role models for masculine and feminine behavior, their behavior often leads to ridicule and rejection among their peers. This results in a further sense of alienation from their masculine or feminine identity.

Many who have experienced a lack of emotional bonding with their father or mother can be driven to the quest of dysfunctional sex-identified behavior. As puberty sets in, this examination begins to zero in on the physical evidence of sexuality in the school changing rooms, on TV, or at the movies. This is where pornography can be particularly damaging. In the subconscious search to find a role model or a gender identity, some teenagers

---

25   Frank Worthen, *Helping People Step Out of Homosexuality*, 1995.

find themselves looking at members of their gender in the changing rooms or in the sex scenes at the movies, more so than the opposite sex—a behavior that convinces them all the more that they must be homosexual.

Even if these teens succeed in mimicking proper behavior for their gender, they still sense that something is missing. They are still not fully identified with their peers, particularly as it relates to their behavior toward and desire for the opposite sex. As a result, emotional needs become sexualized, and they naturally begin to confuse the emotional pull toward members of their sex with their emerging sexual drive. Again, not every young person strives to be accepted by those of their gender. Many are driven toward opposite-sex relationships, and they can confuse the need for emotional intimacy with addictive sexual pleasure.

The Father's Role

Over the years of counseling and talking with other colleagues, I've come to believe that one of the major root causes of sexual and relational problems is a deep fear of abandonment, a fear that begins in childhood. Fathers have always been considered as the protector of the family. An abusive father betrays his God-intended purpose in the family. Other members of the family then fear and mistrust him, and his ability to protect the family is lost. Many children come to think of this as normal behavior.

On the other hand, an indifferent father can be even more damaging than an abusive father. He, too, has abdicated his God-given role as a father, and as a result, the child comes to believe that the father does not care for or love them. In today's world, many fathers believe their role is simply to provide for the family while the mother raises the children. The father's involvement is only to assert his power or control. This emotional abandonment can have just as much effect as an absent father.

However, there is one important difference between an indifferent and an absent father. When the father is absent, the child can believe whatever they want to believe about him. When the father is present and indifferent to the child's needs, the evidence is there, and the wounds often go much deeper because the proof cannot be ignored.

In both cases, the child feels rejected and abandoned. These feelings will often be buried, only to surface later in adult life through addictions or other dysfunctional behavior. Such self-destructive behaviors often indicate a deep soul wound that has never been properly healed.

If children are not taught necessary skills or behaviors and are not adequately protected against harm, they often create a fantasy world to protect themselves against the outside world. Children work hard to escape the pain of rejection and the fear of abandonment.

Masturbation at an early age can be one way of soothing that pain and fear. Any action used to cover pain can easily become an addiction. For many young men, masturbation becomes compulsive just after puberty. It becomes their primary source of comfort in times when the disconnection from their fathers is too difficult to deal with.

The Mother's Role

Both sons and daughters also need the role model of the mother; they need to feel nurtured and cared for. However, there is a delicate balance in these relationships. The most common problem that arises in many mother-son relationships is one of interdependence. If the mother does not have a healthy, fully rounded, spiritual, emotional, and physical/sexual relationship with her husband, she can use the son as a surrogate husband, often without knowing it. Some call this "emotional incest" as the mother tries to draw from the son what she is not receiving from her husband. Often, the son will react in very dysfunctional ways that will carry over into his adulthood.

Other boys contend with an over-controlling, and sometimes manipulative mother who thinks she is helping the son because the father is not "doing his job." Many boys in this situation begin to dislike women, but they are caught in a love/hate relationship because they do desire that nurturing, loving relationship with their mother. Some men are drawn into an addiction with prostitutes because this is one way they can be in total control over a woman. They fear any strong woman who could control or dominate them as their mother did in those earlier years.

Many boys, due to the indifference of the father, will cling to the mother for love, affirmation, and acceptance. They desperately want their father to hold, kiss, and love them, yet their father does not meet their legitimate needs. In most cases, the father has learned this behavior from his father and knows no other way of relating to his son. Many of us are victims of this crippling generational pattern. As a result, the son begins to model his life after his mother. He copies the way his mother acts, talks, and moves, and the bond is made stronger. His peers soon sense a difference in him and begin to make fun of him. Since he is not like the other males, he is excluded from the group and feels isolated and once again rejected.

This can also happen when a female child is emotionally disconnected from her mother and develops a strong bond with her father. This in itself is not dysfunctional. It becomes abnormal when she begins to cut herself off from her feminine side and other women around her. Depending on the relationship with her mother, this can also cause great resentment and anxiety that will expose itself in later life.

When emotional pain is buried and not dealt with, it will emerge sooner or later in adolescence or adulthood. Do you remember those old black-and-white horror films where you would often see someone walking through a graveyard at night? Suddenly, a rotten, decaying hand would pop up from the ground and reach out to grab them, resulting in shrieks of horror from the audience. This is exactly what happens when we allow unresolved pain to fester away in our spirits; the pain lies unseen until that deadly hand reaches out to snatch us back into the midst of an emotional nightmare.

The Role of Our Peers

I must agree with Frank Worthen, who says peer rejection plays a major role in affirming a child's "unacceptability." Children who are different are often denied access to the inner circle. They find themselves on the outside looking in, longing to be accepted and included but never quite sharing in the secrets and camaraderie of the group.

Many children will choose isolation to save themselves from the possible rejection of their peers. But from this place of isolation comes more fantasy, leading the child to envy those they see as receiving positive approval from the group. The ones who are accepted become something of an idol, an unhealthy role model as the child feels insignificant and unworthy in comparison to the one who "has it all figured out."

Many men become fixated on the qualities they see in others and want for themselves. For example, they might think the most popular person in a group is more intelligent or physically attractive than they are. This leads to feelings of inadequacy and an urge to emulate or copy that person. Leanne Payne calls this a cannibalistic compulsion. We are driven to become as good as or better than the other person. What is cannibalized is the ability to initiate relationships without fear or the ability to maintain our self-worth without comparing ourselves with others. Without open communication and trust in relationships and a two-way acceptance, there is no true intimacy, only shame and the fear of rejection.

During normal development in puberty, sexual desire emerges. If a child or teenager already looks up to and admires someone of the same sex, the idolization can easily gain sexual overtones; this often feels natural as feelings progress from a simple desire to one that mingles with emerging sexual feelings.

Many teenagers are now taught that their emerging feelings are proof of homosexuality and that this is perfectly natural and okay. Once tested, they may receive the gender acceptance that their emotional side has been crying out for. The conclusion is then all too easily made: that they were designed to be homosexual and that this is the only way their deepest needs can be met.

In today's permissive society, opposite-sex experiences in puberty are often accepted and condoned as normal. Biblically, the Word is very clear that any sexual activity outside the boundaries of marriage is a rebellion against God's original intent for His creation.

The Woman at the Well

I like the story of the Samaritan woman in John 4:1–42. It represents all of us who are broken. Many of us have grown up believing God is a hard taskmaster, a legalistic judge who is more than ready to condemn. However, when I read this passage, I see all over again that Jesus, who is God Himself, went out of His way to meet this woman at her place of need (verse 4).

In all my rebellion, guilt, and shame, I never thought for one second that God would pursue me! I believed God had turned His back on me, and to get his attention I would have to do something drastic. I didn't have the strength or courage to reach out to Him, and neither did the Samaritan woman, but Jesus went out of His way to meet with her.

This is what I learned. First, the Jews of those days hated the Samaritans and normally would have nothing to do with them. Second, in those days, men simply did not associate with women, let alone talk to them on a personal level. Third, besides being a Samaritan and a woman, she was also an adulteress, making her the lowest of the low in society at that time.

Jesus met this woman at noon, the hottest time of the day. The respectable women of the town would come to the well in the mornings, when it was cool to draw water; however, this woman could only come in the middle of the day because the other women did not accept her.

This story tells of this woman who met Jesus personally. As he talked with her, Jesus showed that He knew all about her previous sins, and yet He did not condemn her; rather, He gave insight into the circumstances she found herself in. Jesus spoke in such a way that she realized her need, and He presented her with a choice. He told her, "If you only knew what a wonderful gift God has for you, and who I am, you would ask me for some living water!" With the offer made, it was up to her to make the next move. Jesus had seen what nobody else could see in her: the potential for life, healing, and freedom from her sins.

Like many of us, she knew *about* the Messiah but did not *know* Him personally. Jesus went out of His way to meet her and presented her with the truth of who He was. As soon as her heart was opened, she took action and reached out for the life He offered.

The story continues in John 4:28:

Then the woman left her waterpot beside the well and went back to the village and told everyone, 'Come and meet a man who told me everything I ever did! Can this be the Messiah?' So the people came streaming from the village to see him.

Because people heard, they acted. And because they also met Jesus *personally*, they could make their own decisions.

The Process of Change

Change doesn't happen right away. It is a time-honored process that takes years—indeed, a lifetime. The interesting thing about the process of change in Christianity is that change itself is not our goal. Change is what happens naturally as we pursue a far more important and compelling goal: knowing, loving, and observing Jesus.

As we walk out of our brokenness, we sometimes focus too intently on our inner hang-ups, past hurts, and sinful tendencies. Looking inward, we may be overcome by the sinfulness of our hearts and begin to despair. However, release and healing come when we recognize the sinful nature of our hearts and then reach up to the One who can help us through that process of change. The cry of our heart becomes, "God, I want to know You. I want to love and worship You. I want to be a man or woman who reflects Your image. Cleanse me from everything that stands between You and me." God delights in such a prayer.

God has given us all that great power of choice. With that power, we can build or destroy, bless or curse, give life or destroy life. Change is a cooperative venture between

God and ourselves, through the power of the Holy Spirit. By His grace, we are invited to come to Him, and then He empowers us to make the right choices.

A True Image of God

Many of us have a distorted view of God, which makes it exceedingly difficult for us to trust Him, let alone other people. Those who have been abused find it particularly difficult to trust God in the sensitive areas of sexuality and identity. Often, we confuse the character of God with that of an abusing or disappointing authority figure in our past. In such cases, we need to confess our feelings to God and ask Him to heal us of this misconception. He is faithful to do this in ways that personally speak to and reassure us.

Over the years, I've seen many people climb out of sexual or relational addictions, while others remain in their brokenness. What is the difference between those who break free and those who don't? The issue of control seems to be the deciding factor. Those who decide to follow Christ and do *His will* at any cost are the ones who make it. A surrender is an act of faith and a lifelong commitment to the God we love.

In surrendering our lives to God, there are two choices we must make. We permit God to work in our life as He pleases, and we decide to trust Him in the middle of our life circumstances, believing He is working through them for our ultimate good. Surrender means giving our lives to Christ and trusting the return will be far greater than a life lived under our control:

Likewise you also, reckon yourselves to be dead indeed to sin, but alive to God in Christ Jesus our Lord (Romans 6:11).

Author C. S. Lewis once said, "Fallen man is not simply an imperfect creature who needs improvement, he is a rebel who must lay down his arms." In other words, God is calling for unconditional surrender. The process of our change to wholeness requires deep emotional healing and a restructuring of our whole identity. God can only do this if we step out of the driver's seat and allow Him to take over with our consent and cooperation.

Surrender is an issue of trust, and trust is built on relationship. To trust God fully, we must work on our relationship with Him. As we walk through life with Him, we begin to know and trust Him to an ever-greater degree, allowing Him into the deepest areas of our lives.

However, when God calls us to this kind of commitment, we often struggle to hold on to just one thing from the past. Sometimes we don't even know what that one thing is, but it creates an unseen barrier, holding us back from total surrender and true intimacy with God. Perhaps that one thing is pride, or fear, or a single behavior we determine to keep for ourselves since we have given everything else to God. If we want true release from our fears and hurts, we must give up this one thing that we hold so dear. God must have access into every area of our lives.

Some of us fear what God might do; for example, He might ask us to share our deepest struggles with someone else. We fight and kick against Him, firmly resisting God's challenge to commit to Him at a deeper level than ever before. However, once we make that final decision to let go, it marks a major turning point in our lives. It won't bring instant release, but it opens up the way for God to begin working in our hearts and lives at a much deeper level.

Have you ever given God specific permission to work in every area of your life, including your sexuality? I suggest you write down any fears you have about this decision, then take a look at what you've written. Seeing our thoughts in black and white often helps us to recognize and accept the need for change.

Total surrender is important; we must obey God one step at a time in the process of recovery, often not understanding His methods but trusting Him for the outcome. For some, this may mean opening up for the first time to another individual regarding their sexual brokenness. Most feel this is impossible because of their position in the church or community or fear of losing their families, friends, and possibly their jobs. These are legitimate concerns, but we all need support and encouragement from others. There is tremendous power in a mutual confession of our weaknesses; through this, we understand everyone shares the same need for Christ:

> But if we [really] are living and walking in the Light, as He [Himself] is in the Light, we have [true, unbroken] fellowship with one another, and the blood of Jesus Christ His Son cleanses (removes) us from all sin and guilt [keeps us cleansed from sin in all its forms and manifestations]. (1 John 1:7, Amplified)

Most of us know that the longer something is kept secret, the more power it has over our lives. A good example is when a person is molested as a child. They often feel ashamed and guilty, and that shame becomes the lock on the door of their secret. If the heart issues are not dealt with, they may grow up to become abusers themselves.

We must also acknowledge God's sovereignty and lordship in our lives, which means trusting Him for the right timing in our recovery. Sometimes His timing will seem quite different from our own. We may want God to do everything now, but in His sovereign will, He knows what is best for us and how much we can cope with at each stage of the healing process. God is looking for eternal change—a heart that has learned through experience to stand strong in a storm. A stone wall may take longer to build, but it can stand for centuries, while a wooden fence may be built in days but only lasts for a few short years.

Each of us is different, and God deals with us in specific and personal ways. Consider Jesus's miracles of healing in the Bible; in almost every case, we hear nothing of what happens to the person afterward as they're integrated back into society.

In 1 Peter, we read:

He Himself bore our sins in His body on the cross, that we might die to sin and live to righteousness; for by His wounds, you were healed. For you were continually straying like sheep, but now you have returned to the Shepherd and Guardian of your souls (1 Peter 2:24–25, NAS).

Many who came to Jesus were healed, but the process of change after years of confusion and deception will take time.

The process of change can be painful, and we grow impatient with it, wanting to get over the pain and move into a brighter season. Leaders in the church may fall into this trap when counseling others, wanting them to move on quickly into total healing. The fact is that many of us don't want to see the pain in others because it reminds us of our unresolved wounds.

At times in the healing process, we may struggle with intense rage, sorrow, or jealousy even though we are progressing wonderfully. God has simply waited until we have developed a solid level of trust in Him before allowing these emotions to surface; this is all part of the healing process.

On the Road to Change

There are several things we can do to kickstart or maintain God's program of change in our lives. The following are a few key methods of moving forward.

The first is practicing God's presence—that is, quieting ourselves before God, resting in Him, and enjoying His fellowship. As we read in Psalm 46:10, "Be still, and know that I am God."

Spend quality time with God Himself, resting in His presence rather than bringing your list of requests and complaints. Sometimes just resting before Him is all we need, and He has already heard the cry of our hearts.

We also need to listen for the healing Word of God. As

we listen to Him speaking in the quiet places of our hearts, we discover our true identity in Christ.

The second is praying for ourselves. We need to be honest with God. He is not shocked by confessions of involvement in masturbation, pornography, or other sexual sins. Nothing we do or say is a surprise to Him, but confessing those sins is the only way to forgiveness:

> *If we confess our sins, He is faithful and righteous to forgive us our sins and to cleanse us from all unrighteousness. If we say that we have not sinned, we make Him a liar, and His word is not in us (1 John 1:9–10, NAS).*

We all need a clean start every day, free from the weight of condemnation from the past. If we start with a clean slate each day, the enemy has no grounds or rights to accuse us. We need to bring our sins to God as He convicts us of the need for change. The difference between conviction and condemnation is that when we are *convicted* of sin, we feel remorse about our actions, and we are drawn to the mercy and forgiveness of Christ. However, in *condemnation*, we feel accused and guilty, with no chance of pardon or change.

One idea for a practical means of encouragement is to keep a large glass jar near your bed. Every time God answers a specific prayer, drop a colored marble into the jar and watch the mounting evidence of God's interest and involvement in your life.

The third avenue of change is praying for others. Pray

for those who are still struggling. Turn your concerns into prayer requests. We tend to be so focused on our problems that we lose sight of the struggle of others around us. Take a moment every day to focus your thoughts on others, and you'll find your problems are being dealt with in the meantime by the Holy Spirit.

A fourth avenue is praise and worship. The Bible tells us that God inhabits the praises of His children. Those who love being in the presence of God and simply enjoying Him are those who are most likely to walk away from sexual addiction, homosexuality, or relational idolatry. These things simply cannot compare with a truly intimate relationship with Christ.

Fifth, great power is found in studying the Bible, which is, after all, God's blueprint for life. Make an effort to personalize the scriptures, reading them as if they were written for you alone. Then try to apply those words to your life. Although it is helpful to read and even memorize verses, application is the key. Just as a seed can't produce fruit until it is planted and breaks open in the ground, so the seed of God's Word can't produce fruit until it is firmly planted in our lives.

The sixth avenue of change is journaling. Recording your thoughts in a journal is an excellent way of tracking your progress. Take time to record your emotions and impressions of what God is doing in your life. At times when the road gets rough and you begin to doubt, you can always look back and see the evidence that God is at work. A journal is particularly helpful when you don't have anyone to confide in, and it offers a wonderful opportunity to build intimacy with God.

At the same time, a journal is no substitute for a trained counselor if you are struggling with difficult issues in your life. We all need a helping hand at times, and another person can help you to see things in perspective.

I have found that there are three common interrelated characteristics in people who come out of a sexually or relationally broken background. The first is the extent of their separation from their worldly support network, the second is the quality of their involvement with a local church, and the third is clear accountability to one or more leaders and strong, healthy Christian friends. Unless your relationship with other Christians becomes and remains stronger than your former relationships, you will probably return to a sexually broken world.

Addictive, compulsive, sexual, or homosexual behavior is overcome by God's power, just like any other sin. But one fact remains: we must agree with God and surrender to His will to see the full impact of change in our lives.

In Matthew 18, Jesus states:

"Again I say to you, that if two of you agree on earth about anything that they may ask, it shall be done for them by My Father who is in heaven" (Matthew 18:19, NAS).

We need to agree with the Word of God, which says we can do anything with the strength God gives. All too often, we listen to the voice of our hearts (our past experiences), the negative voices of our friends, or even the voice of the enemy, which says we can't succeed, or we'll never be any good, and we agree with them.

I have used this scripture many times to agree with disciples about their healing and the promises of God for their life. All through the Word, we find the Holy Spirit pointing out the importance of agreement, unity. We've always thought of that agreement as for our spiritual good. It seems to me that agreement can go either way, positive or negative, and "it will be done for them."

When we go through a rough patch or are tempted, many of the old tapes within us begin to play. These are usually negative experiences, many of which are rooted in our childhood, that have been cemented into our belief system and are what we have come to believe about ourselves. Then another voice, our enemy the devil, agrees with those experiences. At that point, our spirit has a choice to agree with the tapes and the voice, or we can agree with the voice of God and His Word to us about us. We have the power to choose to *agree* with God or with the voices that speak to us to tempt and/or condemn.

Check out the times you agreed with the tapes and/or the voice. What happened? Was "it done"? Or did you agree with God and His Word about you? What was the result of your choice to agree with God?

The wrong friends can have a negative influence on the healing process as well, but God uses the right people to build powerfully into our lives. He has established the local church as a place for healing and interpersonal support, a safe place for people to share their weaknesses and encourage each other toward growth and healing. This principle is clearly stated in Hebrews 10:25:

> *Let us not give up meeting together, as some are in the habit of doing, but let us encourage one another.*

The Bible encourages us to link ourselves with other Christians. This is especially vital for the man or woman coming out of homosexuality, and it places a huge responsibility on the church and church leadership to provide a safe place for those who desire change. The church should be a place where those who need healing can receive support and wise godly counsel concerning their struggles. It is important that they are not shamed into change but surrounded by those who admit their struggles and encourage them to continue in "the good fight of faith."

Many of us would be surprised at the positive reaction of our pastors if we opened up to them. There are exceptions; some church leaders will react from their brokenness and won't want to know about your problems, but these leaders are a minority. It's important to build up your relationship with God and then trust the Holy Spirit to guide you to someone you can trust for help with your struggles.

In Matthew 18:3, Jesus says that unless we become like little children, we will never enter the kingdom of heaven. In verses 5 to 7, he also says great wrath is in store for anyone who leads his children astray. When I first read this passage, I felt Jesus was talking only to abusers of children. However, over the past eleven years, I've come to understand there are many different types of abuse: physical, sexual, mental, verbal, and spiritual. We are all God's children, and if anyone abuses us in any way, including those in church leadership, God will one day call them to account for their actions.

Over time, you will also find many in the body of Christ who will genuinely care for you and accept you as a brother or sister in Christ, regardless of the issues you are struggling with. All these initiatives are stepping-stones on the road to healing. The process of change is, in some ways, a lifelong commitment; even those who break free of sexual addiction still have the tail ends of issues to deal with. It takes the church and everyone in it to support the healing process within each other. We all need each other.

In saying this, we must not forget that our greatest support and encouragement comes from the Lord Himself:

> *Blessed be the God and Father of our Lord Jesus Christ, the Father of mercies and God (Who is the source) of all comfort (help and encouragement), who comforts (helps and encourages) us in all our tribulation (trouble, calamity, and affliction), that we may be able to comfort (help and encourage) those who are in any trouble, with the comfort (help and encouragement) with which we ourselves are comforted (helped and encouraged) by God.*
> *(2 Corinthians 1:3–4, Amplified)*

If you've struggled with secret sins, you'll know that at times, despair creeps in, and you doubt the power of God to bring complete healing and restoration to your life. At such times, you need to know God has promised a bright future for you as long as your heart is inclined toward Him:

For I know the thoughts that I think toward you, says the LORD, thoughts of peace and not of evil, to give you a future and a hope (Jeremiah 29:11).

These words were written by Jeremiah to the Jews in Babylon after they were taken captive by King Nebuchadnezzar. Life looked very bleak for the Jews at that time; their nation had been plundered, many of their friends and loved ones had been killed, and they were prisoners in a foreign land. However, during these terrible circumstances, God gave a message of hope. He had great plans for them, just as He does for you and me. Although the timing of it may not make sense, hold on to that promise. One day, at exactly the right time, all the pieces will fall into place, and you'll see the redemptive hand of God at work in your life.

God did not forget His people, even though they were held captive in Babylon for seventy years. This stage of captivity was all part of His plan for them—a plan to rebuild Jerusalem and the Jewish people as a nation. In times of deep trouble, it may seem like God has forgotten you. But God may be preparing you, as He did the people of Judah, for a brand-new beginning.

Some are afraid of God because of His awesome and unlimited power. Others mistrust Him and are suspicious He wants to harm them in some way. Some leaders struggle with these issues but are afraid to confide in anyone in case they lose all they have worked so hard to achieve. But scripture tells us God loves us and wants only the absolute best for us. His heart toward us is echoed in the words penned by Jeremiah: "God's plans are for good, for peace and prosperity." If you are God's child, you have nothing to fear. Like a loving Father, God has a glorious future planned for you, if only you will turn the steering wheel of your life over to Him.

God knows the future He has planned for us. Our response must be to trust Him and live by faith, like a child holding her father's hand. The Father knows the way, and the way is good; our role is simply to trust in Him and follow His lead.

It's easy to feel like one ridiculously small fish in the sea when you consider all of the billions on earth. Yet no matter what your status is in the world, God is thinking about you even now and making plans for your life. You are important to Him.

Although God promises to bless His children, that doesn't mean He will shower us with wealth or eliminate all suffering and hardship from our lives. We live in a sinful world, so we must contend with the effects of sin and with sinful people. Suffering is part of what it means to be human. But God's prosperity goes beyond this life for those who know Him. So, when you are struggling through difficult circumstances, take heart! God has much greater things in store for us in heaven!

"Open your eyes and look at the fields,
because they are ready for harvest."

John 4:34b (CSB)

For more information about
Restoring Wholeness, go to:

RestoringWholeness.org

Made in the USA
Las Vegas, NV
12 April 2022